What About
KANSAS CITY!

What About KANSAS CITY!

A HISTORICAL HANDBOOK

Dory DeAngelo

TWO LANE PRESS, INC.

Also by Dory DeAngelo:

Voices Across Time, Profiles of Kansas City's Early Residents
The Plaza, Kansas City's World Famous Shopping Center
Kansas City Style, A Social and Cultural History of Kansas City, As Seen Through Its Lost Architecture (Co-author)
Passages Through Time, Stories About Kansas City, Missouri, And Its Northeast Neighborhood

First printing October 1995

ISBN: 1-878686-19-4

Printed in the United States of America

Cover design: Jim Langford
Photo on page 98: Bob Barrett
Photo on page 147: David Remley
Editing: Jane Doyle Guthrie

10 9 8 7 6 5 4 3 2 1 95 96 97 98 99

For special sales or academic orders contact:

Two Lane Press, Inc.
4245 Walnut Street
Kansas City, Missouri 64111

CONTENTS

PREFACE

Some people believe that history is a never-ending parade of people and events; others believe that the process just keeps repeating itself, going around and around like a carousel.

I'm inclined toward the "what goes around comes around" theory. In researching through newspapers dating back over a hundred years, over and over I've seen disasters to cope with, new buildings to construct, great celebrations to enjoy, horrendous crimes that call for justice, and incredible kindness and compassion shown toward those less fortunate.

Maybe the characteristics of wanting to build things and celebrate successes and help others is part of our genetic makeup. If genes carry our heritage, not only from our parents but from the first human being, then maybe they **are** the carousel. Each one of us is along for the ride for our limited lifespans. As the carousel goes around, the scenery is new to the latest group of riders but it has all happened before.

FROM THE PUBLISHER

The publisher offers a special thank you to Siusan Cox, a seasoned bookseller in the Kansas City area, for her role in the development of this project. Siusan's awareness of empty "niches" on her shelves and her responsiveness to her customers' interests provided the impetus for publishing this delightful collection of local history.

ACKNOWLEDGMENTS

This history could not have been written without the help of those who wrote about Kansas City in the past and those who collected their writings. There are several historic archives and collections in the metropolitan area, plus many individuals who have researched their own family's history have added to the collective history of this area.

The majority of information for this book was gathered at the Missouri Valley Special Collections section of the downtown Kansas City, Missouri, Public Library. The staff there as always was most helpful and cooperative. The photos in this book, except where indicated, are from MVSC's extensive historic photo collection.

With deep appreciation for her life-long friendship
I dedicate this book to Jacqueline Royal Cumberford.

Note that in the early days of Kansas City, certain streets either had no name, or had names that are no longer in use. For clarity's sake, I have put today's street names on locations that are written about here.

A CITY CARVED BY ICE AND WATER

The Ice Age had as much to do with the birth of Kansas City as did the trappers, traders, and early pioneers. For billions of years, ice caps, sometimes a mile thick, covered most of the earth's Northern Hemisphere, then one solid mass of land. Almost all of what would become Missouri was covered at least twice by continental ice sheets. As the glaciers rolled over the earth, they pushed along boulders and deposits of clay, sand, and gravel. Layer upon layer of this debris was propelled into the Missouri area. These materials are responsible for the rich farmland and the diversity of rock formations— rolling hills, high bluffs, and mountains—that sets the state apart from the flat landscape of the western prairie.

About 200 million years ago, the large landmass began to separate into continents and what would become North America moved closer to the equator. Along with the push and shove of the glaciers, wind and erosion cut out valleys, hundreds of feet deep, that captured frozen water. During warm-up periods, the ice lakes melted and large expanses of surging water spilled through the center of North America. This inland sea, sometimes referred to as the Kansas-Nebraska Sea, flowed from the Arctic Ocean south to the Gulf of Mexico, covering today's Kansas City. It left many fossils, including those of ancient marine life that are embedded in the limestone rocks around the city. These small fossils are visible today in the high bluffs called Cliff Drive, overlooking the river in the Northeast section of the city. The ice and water also created many underground springs throughout the city and formed many large limestone caves underneath the city and surrounding areas. This system of caves, because they maintain the same temperatures year round, make Kansas City a leader in the underground storage industry.

The water that became the Missouri River originally flowed south from the North Pole ice cap near Hudson Bay, entering Missouri just south of today's Iowa state line. The water then traveled east to empty into the Atlantic Ocean. During one of the last freezes, however, the ice cap pushed the river channel farther south and put a bend in it where it met the Kansas (or Kaw) River, just west of today's downtown Kansas City. Here the combined waters turn east to flow toward the Mississippi. This bend and the natural rock levee carved by the ice (where Grand Avenue now meets the river) sealed the fate of Kansas City. The levee was ideal for steamboat landings.

The Missouri River is the second longest river in the country. (The Mississippi is approximately 35 miles longer.) The Missouri begins in southwestern Montana at 4,032 feet above sea level, where three rushing mountain streams unite to form a single river. As the waters flow south across today's North and South Dakota and Nebraska, various smaller rivers and streams, draining an area of nearly 600,000 miles, contribute to the volume and strength of the river. In some areas the Missouri River is a mile wide.

When the ice melts in the spring or there is a summer of steady rain, overflowing tributaries upstream empty into the Missouri River and it overflows into ancient dry channels. Then water covers the lowlands all along the river's banks as it has for thousands of years. Although the river has been dredged to make it wider and deeper, and several dams have been built along the river's path to control flooding, almost every year the Missouri breaks through all barriers. Every flood seems to prove that man cannot tame the waters of the Mighty Missouri.

When the first recorded flood occurred in 1826, there was only Chouteau's trading post, on the north bank of the river to wash away. The flood of June 14, 1844, reported to be Kansas City's worst, had more to destroy. Sixty consecutive days of rain brought the river to a crest of 48 feet, judged by the high-water mark on the bluffs north of the river. The French settlement on the river's southern bank, all of what was then Kansas City, was swept away except for one brick warehouse.

The 1903 flood was the combined waters of the Missouri and Kaw and crested at 38 feet. The city's population had reached over 160,000, and buildings and homes had expanded into the flood plain. The Northeast Industrial district, where the French settlement had been, was covered with water. Homes and businesses built along rivers and creeks were washed away. The flood destroyed 16 of the 17 railroad bridges crossing the Missouri and Kaw Rivers, and with the Union Depot under water, all railroad traffic was stalled. The stockyards and meat-packing plants were flooded out. Twenty people were killed and more than 22,000 were left homeless. The city's water supply was contaminated. And with 225 saloons in the flooded districts being forced to close, there wasn't even a beer to drink.

The Missouri and Kaw Rivers have continued to overflow almost every year. Some years brought more damage and some less, but only a few floods made history. The deluges of 1951, 1977, and 1993 were called "100-year floods" and even "500-year floods."

Union Street in the West Bottoms was covered with water in the 1903 flood. The Union Depot at left was flooded, and trains couldn't get in or out. This prompted planning for the Union Station.

The flood of July 13, 1951, was called "Black Friday." That summer had brought 40 days of steady rain to Kansas and Missouri. The Kaw River and its tributaries were overflowing. On July 12, river dikes were breached in Manhattan, Topeka, and Lawrence. The muddy water gained breadth and speed as it moved closer to Kansas City. At midmorning, on Friday, July 13, whistles in factories in the West Bottoms started sounding the alarm. At 11 a.m., an estimated 500,000 cubic feet of water pushed through the floodwalls on the Missouri side of the Kaw into the West Bottoms industrial district. The water threatened the lives of over 12,000 people who lived and worked there and had not heeded the flood warnings.

As the 15-foot-high wall of water began rolling into the area, thousands of people took what belongings they could and rushed to get out, in cars, trucks, trailers, taxis, and even streetcars. The vehicles clogged every bridge and viaduct leading out of the Bottoms to the Quality Hill bluffs above. There was such a traffic jam that people soon abandoned their vehicles and started running to safety as the water climbed up the viaducts. Later, the National Guard manned boats to rescue those who

Looking down into the West Bottoms from Quality Hill at the viaducts engulfed by the 1951 flood water. Cars can be seen stranded on the viaducts.

hadn't been quick enough and were stranded on vehicles or marooned on the top floors or roofs of buildings.

The force of the water sweeping along picked up large metal storage tanks and tossed them like toys. A 6,000-gallon tank partially filled with diesel fuel was pushed down the swift canal that was Southwest Boulevard. Only a few blocks from downtown Kansas City the tank collided with a high-voltage line, exploded near a bulk gasoline storage area, and ignited several gasoline storage tanks containing thousands of gallons of fuel. The fire soon encompassed eight blocks. The flames and black clouds of smoke rose so high that they could be seen throughout the metropolitan area. WDAF-TV, located at 31st and Summit just above the explosion, covered the $10 million fire below all day with cameras mounted on the roof of their building.

The powerful water loosened four large barges from their moorings on the riverbank, carrying them toward the Hannibal railroad bridge and the A.S.B. Bridge. (The latter was replaced in the 1990s by the Heart of America Bridge.) Luckily, the barges passed under the bridges without doing serious damage. Water also crept into the southern part of North Kansas City, causing evacuation there, too. High water and swift current were eroding the earth around the perimeters of the Fairfax industrial district and the Municipal Airport. Preparing for the worse, volunteers came from everywhere and worked straight through the night to shore up the dikes with sandbags.

The hard work paid off. At 3 a.m. the next morning the Missouri River crested at 38 feet. The sandbags had kept the water from the airport and the Fairfax district.

The 1951 flood damage was estimated at $900 million. Three people were killed, 4,725 homes were damaged, and 17,550 people were evacuated from in the flooded areas. Businesses also were damaged or destroyed. Many large companies, such as Hallmark Cards, had warehouses in the West Bottoms that suffered heavy damage. Since the flooding had contaminated water systems, there was a shortage of drinking water throughout the whole metropolitan area. People called this a 100-year flood, meaning it could only happen every 100 years, but it took only 26 years for a record-breaking deluge to again devastate Kansas City.

Floods here were supposed to only happen in the lowlands, not in the very heart of the city. But September 12, 1977, floodwater damaged many parts of southern Kansas City and destroyed portions of the city's pride and joy: The Country Club Plaza.

Many do not realize that the land The Plaza is built on was once a swamp fed by waters from Brush Creek on the south and Mill Creek on the east. Now just a street name, Mill Creek was once a stream running from Westport south through the Plaza land to join Brush Creek at today's Main Street. Mill Creek dried up, the banks of Brush Creek were shored up, and the area was filled in with solid earth that would support the construction of Plaza buildings.

Before the redesign of Brush Creek in 1993, just a trickle of water was in the creek bed during dry seasons. But when various creeks in Wyandotte and Johnson Counties flood, volumes of water moved through the creek with incredible speed and depth. In 1936, to protect The Plaza, a portion of Brush Creek was paved over. East of Main Street, underground pipes were laid to handle the overflow and speed it east into the Little Blue River, which travels northeast through populated areas to empty into the Missouri just beyond I-435.

The cause of the September 1977 flood was heavy localized rainfall that metrologists called a 100-year probability. On Monday, September 12, in a 12-hour period, 16 inches of rain drenched the metropolitan area, particularly south of the Missouri River. By that afternoon, water was backed up all along the Blue River from the Missouri River south to

95th street, flooding out businesses and homes. At some points the Blue was 49 feet high; it could not handle the runoff from Brush Creek. Having nowhere else to go, the creek ran over its normal boundaries into The Plaza.

Even though the National Weather Service put out dangerous flood warnings on radio and television at 8:30 p.m., it was inconceivable that The Plaza could flood. Activity went on there as usual, as if nothing could happen. At 11:30 Brush Creek, then 15-to 20-feet high, spilled over its banks. High water moved into the streets and buildings on the south side of The Plaza.

People eating their dinners at Plaza restaurants just two blocks north of Brush Creek wanted to finish dessert before they left. There wasn't time. Water from Brush Creek rushed through the front doors of the restaurants and was waist high before guests could clean their plates. Waiters and busboys formed a human chain to help diners through the water and out the back doors to safety. The force of the flood caved in shop windows. Parked cars were not only swept into trees and windows, but wedged under Brush Creek's bridges (later 35 wrecked cars were towed out of the creek). Water blew holes in store walls and carried merchandise miles away. It also caused a fire that destroyed the whole 600 block of 48th Street on the west end of the Plaza.

The destruction to the area's shops, restaurants, and Alameda Hotel, was estimated at $58 million. Although The Plaza was the heaviest hit dollar-wise, this flood killed and also destroyed property in other parts of the city and metropolitan area. Floodwater filled existing creeks as well as ancient dry creek beds, reaching out to snag lives and destroy homes south and east of Brush Creek and in Johnson County. Twenty-five people were killed. Although it was called another 100- year flood, Nature waited only 16 years to break that record.

The next deluge was called a "once in five centuries flood." Unlike the one that hit The Plaza all in one day, the flood of July 1993 was over a year in the making. After years of drought, Missouri, Kansas, Iowa, and Nebraska experienced unusually high amounts of rainfall in 1992, and above-average precipitation continued into 1993. The parched earth soaked it up. Seldom did days pass without rain. From the middle of May to the middle of July in 1993, it rained 40 out of 61 days until the farmlands and lawns couldn't absorb anymore. The runoff added to the already swollen creeks, and they spilled over into the tributaries of the Mississippi, Missouri, and Kaw rivers. Never before in recorded history had these rivers coursed with such volume and power. The rains continued and so did the flooding.

The waters pushed into lowlands, farmland, and river towns, backing up as well in the streets of major cities. Kansas City flooded in the same areas that had been affected for centuries: the West Bottoms, the Leeds industrial area near the Blue River, and the north and south banks of the Missouri River. The old municipal airport across from downtown Kansas City again was threatened. Although merchants on the Plaza feared a repeat of 1977, the deepening of the Brush Creek channel beyond Oak Street kept the water flowing east without doing any damage to the famous shopping district.

As before, water plucked barges away from their secured lines and shoved them into bridges. The *William S. Mitchell*, an old deteriorating paddle wheeler waiting to be restored, was carried from its dock in Kansas City, Kansas, and tossed against the Broadway, Hannibal, and Paseo Bridges. Luckily it did not inflict much damage, but the boat was much the worse for the trip when the water finally released it on the south bank of the Missouri, east of the Paseo Bridge.

In 1918, Turkey Creek was diverted by underground pipes into the Kaw River. But when that river is at flood stage, the creek backs up and spills over its boundaries. This happened in the 1993 flood. Turkey Creek's overflow pushed into the West Bottoms. Water poured into Kemper Arena and the newly completed American Royal Building. The creek's waters also traveled along Kansas City's Southwest Boulevard, reaching eastward almost to the Southwest Trafficway overpass. The boulevard's east section, an area of popular restaurants and businesses, suffered heavy damage.

Parkville and Riverside, two communities across the Missouri River from Kansas City, also were hard hit. Even though 350 volunteers came to sandbag Parkville's riverfront in hopes of keeping the water out of the city's historic downtown, the river leached into part of that shopping district anyway. The commercial district of Riverside, right on the river's edge, was evacuated, and businesses there were flooded out. Homes were evacuated in five counties in the Kansas City area, and 52 federal levees were damaged or destroyed. After the floodwaters receded, residents discovered millions of dollars of damage to the area's highways, including a large section of Interstate 635 near Riverside.

Almost 70,000 people had to evacuate their towns and homes because of the flooding. In river towns up and down the Missouri and

Mississippi, more than 55,000 homes were damaged or destroyed. Although many reclaimed their land, the federal government paid for some towns along the rivers to move their residents and businesses to higher ground. The U.S. Army Corps of Engineers repaired most of the damaged levees along the Missouri, and the Missouri Conservation Commission purchased some of the frequently flooded bottomland to convert it into wetlands, allowing Nature to reclaim it at will.

As devastating as the 1993 flood was, people living in the flood plains areas were hopeful that it wouldn't happen again. They cleaned up the mess and went on about their lives.

The Corps of Engineers worked to widen and deepen Brush Creek from Roanoke Parkway to Troost. The five-year, $87 million project included work on the Blue River that would funnel floodwaters quickly from the creek into the Missouri River. There was more to do on Brush Creek east of Troost and on the Blue, but planners felt there would be time before another flood hit.

However, by the middle of May 1995, a month-long heavy rain in the Heartland soaked the earth and again overflowed the rivers. It was a repeat of 1993. The water from the upper Missouri River and its tributaries pushed into towns along their paths. As the Missouri River met the Kaw at their confluence, water surged into Turkey Creek. The creek again backed up and flooded parts of Southwest Boulevard. As the floodwater traveled east into the Blue River, that body overflowed into the same populated areas along its path. Highways became impassable on both sides of the Missouri River. Flooding continued all along the Missouri's route toward the Mississippi. As in 1993, all of the agricultural levees were breached, flooding farms. River towns that were inundated in 1993 again were threatened, and sandbagging at the edge of these towns once more became a familiar sight.

The 1993 flood was called a "once in five centuries disaster," but two years later it happened again. Nature keeps her own timetable.

CARETAKERS OF THE LAND

Before the first European came to this part of the country, Indians had named the plants, the trees, and the landscape. Many of these names remain in some form today, but since there are no authenticated records of all the early Indian languages, we have only the Spanish and French explorers' phonetic spelling and translations. The English and Americans took these names and gave them their versions, removing them further from the original language.

Indian tribes that inhabited the Mississippi Valley had a variety of names for the Missouri River. The Siouan or Sioux name for the river translated into "river of thick water." The Osage, who like the Missouris were a branch of the Siouan family, called it "smoky river." The Delawares referred to it as "rock river." The Pawnees' name for this river was "mysterious waters." The Wyandots dubbed it "muddy water." The missionary Father Jacques Marquette encountered the Illinois Indians in 1673, and they told him their name for the Missouri River was "Pi-Ki-Tan," meaning "foaming stream." When Marquette came to the confluence of the Mississippi and Missouri Rivers, the swiftness and turbulence of the waters made him decide not to go farther. He decided it thus was well-named and recorded the river as Pekitanoui.

There is no evidence that any of the tribes had a word for Indians in general; instead they described themselves by their tribe's name. Many of the Missouri Valley Indian tribes acquired their present names from what the Illinois Indians, in their eagerness to please, told the French. The Missouris called themselves "Niutachi," which was said to mean "people who dwell at the mouth of a river." However, the Illinois told Marquette that they were called "Miss-Sou-Li-Av," or "canoe men," because they spent so much time on the river in their canoes.

The Kansa Indians had a long history of having their name changed and interpreted. They called themselves "Hutanga," which was suppose to mean "by the edge of the river." It is thought that the name "Kansa" came from Francisco Coronado's 1541 Spanish expedition search for the Seven Cities of Gold. (Coronado came to the plains of Central Kansas, and fragments of Spanish armor have been found near Lyons and Lindsborg, Kansas.) Near today's Junction City, Kansas, the Spanish found a village inhabited by an estimated 25,000 "friendly" Indians. Coronado called the community Quivira. (Today there is a lake by that name in Johnson County, Kansas.) The Quiviras told of a wild band of Indians to the east that frequently tried to raid their village. Although Coronado never saw them, forklore says that the Spanish gave these Indians the name "Cansar," meaning "to exhaust" or "harass" in Spanish. The first known martyrdom for the Catholic faith in this part of the country happened when Padre Juan de Padilla, a member of the Coronado expedition, returned the next year to convert the Quiviras. Reportedly, he was killed by the Cansar Indians.

In 1601 another Spaniard, Juan de Onate, governor of New Mexico, brought a large expedition force from the upper Rio Grande to explore southern Kansas. He found a large village where 600 Indians lived in circular dwellings made of poles covered with tanned hides. He called them "Escansaques." Later the Illinois Indians gave Father Marquette a word that sounded like "Konza" or "Kansa" for a tribe that lived near the confluence of two rivers. They said it meant "south wind people." These Indians carried several names given them by the French: "Ko'n-za," "Canses," and, as early as 1723, " Kaws."

The Osage were related to the Missouris, Kansas, and several other Indian tribes. As part of a large Siouan family of Indians who were thought to have lived in ancient times along the southeast coast of the United States, they shared a common language. At some period in prehistory, the Siouans moved into the Ohio Valley; then, as they migrated farther westward, they separated into various tribes, each one picking out a geographical location as their territory.

The Osage called themselves "Wazhazhe," which they said meant "we are the people." The gossipy Illinois told Marquette this name, but the Frenchman turned it into "Ouazhaghi." When the English arrived on the scene, they anglicized it first to "Ozazge" and then to "Osage."

The names of the earliest Indian tribes who settled in the Kansas City area are unknown. In 1954 an Indian village dated to A.D. 300 was excavated just across the river from downtown Kansas City near Riverside, Missouri. These Indians spent enough time there to plant and harvest. The archeologists dug up pottery still containing pinto beans, charred maize, and small corncobs. They must have either traveled great distances to trade or other tribes came to them with trade goods, because the excavation yielded several copper ornaments from the Great Lake–region Indians and obsidian arrowheads from the Rocky Mountains. These people hunted in the area, as bones of white-tailed deer, coyote, buffalo, beaver, elk, and smaller animals remained in pits at the site. Archeologists identified this place as belonging to "Hopewell Indians."

At the turn of the 20th century, when Kansas City was digging into the earth to build streets and buildings, shovels turned up Indian artifacts at various sites around the city, including 12th and The Paseo, 13th and Vine, and along Cliff Drive in Northeast Kansas City. At the east end of Cliff Drive is a mound that was dug into in 1873 and identified as an Indian burial ground. It is conceivable that the cliffs above the Missouri River were inhabited by Indians called the Middle Mississippians, who built mounds around St. Louis dating to A.D. 800.

Although many different tribes crossed the land that became Kansas City (before and during the forced resettlements in the West), three tribes contributed the most to this city: the Missouris gave the state and river their names, the Kansa gave the city its name, and the Osage gave Kansas City its land.

The Missouris were known by other area tribes as the Ancient Missouris. Although their neighbors along the Missouri River were the Kansa and Osage, they were more closely related to the Otoes and Iowa Indians. Their ability with canoes gave them a reputation as excellent navigators of the Missouri and Mississippi Rivers.

In the early part of the 18th century the Missouris were used by both the French and the Spanish in their struggle to control the middle part of this country. In 1720 the Spaniards sent an expeditionary force from Santa Fe, New Mexico, on the old Indian trail, to join the Pawnees, the Missouris' enemies, to assist in wiping out the Missouris. As the Spaniards grew closer to Missouri, they met a group of warriors who they supposed were Pawnees, but in reality these were Missouris. Not realizing their mistake, they told their new friends of their intent and invited the Indians to spend the night in their camp. The Missouris massacred the Spanish after dark and took their horses. The Plains Indians had the Spanish to thank for introducing them to horses.

When the French heard about the Spanish expedition, they sent Etienne de Bourgmont to establish a fort in the area to protect their interests and their Indian allies. De Bourgmont knew the area because he had completed a survey of the Missouri River to the Platte River in 1713, camping several times near today's Kansas City. His expedition (which included a drummer) left New Orleans in 1723 to travel up the Mississippi and Missouri Rivers and build Fort Orleans, approximately 60 miles east of today's Kansas City, opposite present-day Waverly, Missouri. The only evidence of the fort now is a historic marker.

A large Missouris village was near this fort. The French and

Indians got on well together, and de Bourgmont learned to speak the native's language. He "married" the daughter of the chief and they had a son. (He also later "married" a daughter of an Osage chief and they too had children.) In an effort to form alliances with other tribes, the Frenchman got the Missouris and Osage to travel with him to their other villages to trade horses, guns, swords, hatchets, powder, bullets, and other items. In 1725 de Bourgmont was ordered to return to France and bring chiefs of the major tribes with him. He brought along four Osage and five Missouris (including his wife and son) plus chiefs from the Illinois.

These original Midwesterners were given a royal welcome in Paris. They also went to Fountainbleau to meet 15-year-old King Louis XV, who presented de Bourgmont with a medal on which was carved a naked Indian sitting on a mountain of silver. The Indians became the pets of the French Court. They were taken to the royal garden to demonstrate their ability to stalk and kill a deer. Coats trimmed in gold were tailored for them and masked balls were given in their honor. The Indians gave a dance performance at the Italian Opera House. Women of the court thought the warriors exotic and took them to their bedrooms. The Duchess of Orleans named de Bourgmont's wife the "Princess of the Missouris" and arranged for her to be baptized at Notre Dame Cathedral. Later she arranged a marriage at the Cathedral between the Princess and a Sergeant Dubois who had served with de Bourgmont. The king gave the bride a watch set with diamonds that chimed the hour as a wedding present.

Soon the aristocrats moved on to other interests and the Indians were abandoned. They had to beg for money in order to get back to America. DeBourgmont married a wealthy Parisian widow and lived in France in luxury for the rest of his life. Sergeant and Mrs. Dubois settled at Fort Orleans, but later the Princess returned to her people. It was reported that Dubois was killed in an Indian raid.

Beginning in 1750, the Missouri waged a series of unsuccessful wars with the Sauk and Fox Indians. But the numbers killed in battle couldn't compare to those who succumbed to white men's diseases. By the middle of the 18th century, smallpox had reduced the Missouris from 3,000 to a few hundred. In the 1770s those who survived sickness and warfare traveled to the mouth of the Platte River in Nebraska to join their relatives the Otoes on a reservation. They were absorbed into that tribe. In 1881 the Otoes were relocated west because white settlers wanted their reservation land. By that time, the Missouris, who had been early allies of French exploration and were celebrated on their trip to Paris, had ceased to exist as an individual tribe. The Kansa tribe was never as large or as powerful as the Osage. They did their share of battling with their neighbors. They had a reputation of being cruel to their enemies and sold their captives to the French as slaves to work on Louisiana plantations. When the team of Lewis and Clark were surveying the country west of the Mississippi in 1804, what they saw of the Kansa prompted the surveyors to note in their journal: "dissolute, lawless bandits; frequently plunder their traders and commit depravations on persons ascending and descending the Missouri River."

The French and Spanish both used the Kansa. In June 1724, de Bourgmont brought eight Missouri war chiefs and 100 of their warriors, plus four Osage chiefs and 64 of their warriors, to meet with the Kansa to tell them of the plans to build a fort near the earliest identified Kansa village (north of today's Atchison, Kansas, about 45 miles from Kansas City). After spending two weeks in council, they smoked the peace pipe. In 1744 the French built Fort Cavagnolle above the Missouri River near today's Leavenworth, Kansas. The fort was built not only to trade with the Kansa and protect them, but to make sure Spanish traders could not use the river to trade with other tribes in the area. After the Spanish again gained control of the Louisiana Territory, this fort was abandoned in 1764. A historic marker stands at the site near Fort Leavenworth.

A short time after the Louisiana Purchase was signed, the U.S. government began relocating Indians living east of the Mississippi to Missouri and Kansas Territory. To make a place for them, tribes in the two states had to give up their land. Beginning in 1812, the Kansa signed a series of treaties surrendering their land to make way for these eastern tribes. They first were moved near today's Topeka. In 1845 another treaty took this land and pushed them near Council Grove. In 1873 the surviving 600 Kansa gave up all of their remaining Kansas land and moved to a 100,137-acre reservation in Oklahoma Territory.

The federal government had given the Indian nations rights to all of present-day Oklahoma except the Panhandle. That didn't last long. After the Oklahoma land rush, the government bought back 3 million acres of Indian land, including some of the Kansa property. By the 1880s the Kansa reservation was reduced to a small portion on the Oklahoma-Kansas border. One hundred years later, only 16 full-blooded Kansa remained.

In many respects, the Osage Indians were the most remarkable of all mid-Western tribes. Because they stayed in the same locality longer than any other tribe, they are the oldest tribe in the area for which there are authentic records. (A 2,000 Osage/English dictionary was written in the early 1880s.) Before the white man came, Osage land stretched from the Gulf of Mexico to the Missouri River, and from the Mississippi west to the Rocky Mountains. Unlike the Missouris and the Kansa Indians, the Osage not only survived as a tribe into the 20th century, but their leaders proved to be very crafty dealing with the United States government on land and mineral rights. As a result, in the 1920s the Osage were called some of the wealthiest people in America.

Osage folklore says that for thousands of years their holy men told stories about their origins, calling their ancestors "sky people," who came from the stars to protect the earth. It may be that the "sky people" were those prehistoric men who, 12,000 to 55,000 years ago, crossed the Bering Strait land bridge from Asia to settle the Americas. When the oceans were dammed by the ice caps, sea levels dropped, revealing land usually covered by water. Bands of Asian hunters walked over the connecting land bridge to track down mammoths, mastodons, and other mammals that were the primary meat diet in colder climates. Since these ancient people came from the top of the world, were the Osage stories told about the "sky people" really about the ancestors of all North American Indians?

These primeval people spent some time in the Kansas City area. Beginning in the 1930s, archeologists started finding ancient stone spear heads at a site named Nebo Hill, near today's World's of Fun. The artifacts were later radiocarbon dated to approximately 12,000 years ago.

After the Osage broke away from their Sioux family, they divided into three geographical tribes: the Great or Grand Osage traveled into northern Missouri to settled along the river now called the Grand; the Little Osage, who called themselves "the Children of the Middle Waters," moved into southeastern Missouri, close to the lake country that is now the Lake of the Ozarks; and the third group of Osage settled in Arkansas. The Little Osage's early main village was just 60 miles south of Kansas City. The land was a pie-shaped marsh formed by two rivers that for thousands of years each spring attracted many birds, including cranes, white pelicans, and trumpeter swans, that came there to feed and nest.

The Little Osage had poetry in their naming. They called their ancestral village the "Place of Many Swans." Later the French translated this into Marais des Cygnes —"Swamp of Swans." The land can be seen on today's map of Missouri, formed by the Osage River and the river that the French named Marais des Cygnes. Highway 71 cuts through Osage land, and the town of Rich Hill, Missouri, sits right in the middle of it.

The Osage used several trails in the Kansas City area to visit the Kansa villages to the west and the Saux and Iowa villages to the north. They also traveled on these trails to hunt in the forests along the Missouri River's banks and on their way to annual buffalo hunts. One of their main trails followed today's Highway 71 northwest to the Blue River, where it turned west to connect with Brush Creek. Crossing north again, at approximately Troost Avenue, the path led to the Missouri River. The Indians would take their canoes with them to paddle across the river so they could connect with the Saux trail at Randolph Point near today's World's of Fun.

The Osage not only fought with the nearby Pawnees, but traveled west to battle with migrating tribes such as the Kiowas, the Comanches, the Arapahos, the Cheyennes, and even the Apaches. The Osage and other tribes in the Missouri Valley were given horses, guns and ammunition, and trade goods first by the Spanish, then later by the French and English, to enlist them to fight against Indian enemies of the Long Knives (the native peoples' name for Europeans because they carried swords). The Long Knives also offered payment for scalps of these enemies. (The Osage were called barbarians by the Spanish because they sometimes beheaded captives and put the heads on poles, but early Spanish explorers did the same, if not worse, to the Indians.)

During the War of 1812, English and American representatives came to the Osage and other tribes in the area to ally them against the opposing country. The British promised that they would keep the white settlers out of Indian territory. The Osage took gifts from both sides and even flew a British flag over their village. After the war, William Clark and August Chouteau got the Great and Little Osage chiefs to sign a treaty that not only made perpetual peace between the United States and the Osage nation, but forgave them for any hostile acts against Americans.

This was the same William Clark whom President Jefferson sent with Meriwether Lewis in 1804 to survey west of the Mississippi. This survey started the removal of Indians from their lands. It attracted white settlers west of the Mississippi, who soon wanted Indians out of the way so they could settle the land.

In 1808 the Osage ceded seven-eighths of Missouri and the northern half of Arkansas to the United States. In all, 52.5 million acres were handed over, including the tribe's ancestral village, Place of Many Swans.

One of the Osage chiefs signing the treaty said through an interpreter, "If the Great American Father wanted a part of our land, he must have it. He was rich and powerful; we were poor and pitiful. What could we do?"

The treaty promised to build a fort near the relocated Osage village to protect the tribe from their enemies. This was Fort Osage, sometimes called Fort Clark, located on limestone bluffs above the Missouri River just about 25 miles east of Kansas City.

For their land the Osage received merchandise worth $1,500, a little over $5,000 in cash, farming tools, a blacksmith, and a house for their two main chiefs. Fort Osage was really a sales outlet, and the Osage Indians were the suppliers. Skilled trappers and hunters, they traded their fur pelts for cheap beads, cloth, blankets, knives, hatchets, guns, and ammunition. The fort enjoyed such good business that individuals with their own trading posts felt it had an unfair advantage because the government was involved. They lobbied to close it. Fort Osage was closed in 1822 and dismantled in 1825. The site was restored, however, in a series of restoration projects starting in the 1940s. Today it offers a unique tourist attraction for those who wish to see how life was lived in the early 1800s.

By making the fort a successful operation, the Osage Indians attracted more white men, who in turn would demand the last of their land: a 24-mile strip that would become the heart of Kansas City. In 1825 the remaining 1,789 Osage gave up this tract and moved to the Kansas Indian Territory. They were given $7,000 a year for 20 years, merchandise worth $6,000, hundreds of livestock, and a supply of farming tools, plus their debts to trading stores were paid off. Then the Osage crossed through the Kansas City area for the last time as a tribe, to join 19 other Indian tribes resettled in the Kansas Territory.

White men would later devise a new way to push the Indians onto reservations. White hunters organized massive buffalo hunts (sometimes killing entire herds from moving trains) that almost made the animal extinct. They wanted to eliminate the buffalo because it provided not only the Indians' trade goods but also their food and clothing. Tribes had a choice between starving and freezing to death or moving to reservations. Many who did move to reservations starved to death anyway. Corrupt Bureau of Indian Affairs agents were known to have pocketed monies allocated for their food. By the 1890s almost every tribe in America had their land taken away from them. They were relocated many times, and eventually whole populations were virtually destroyed.

The Osage were also moved several times. They first were settled in the Kansas Territory reservation on a 50-mile-wide piece of land near today's Hutchinson, Kansas. In 1870 the U.S. government needed more land in Kansas for white settlement and agreed to buy the Osage land at $1.25 an acre. They sold it, but unlike other tribes, the Osage didn't allow the government to give them land. They bought 1.47 million acres from the Cherokee Indians for 74 cents an acre in northeastern Oklahoma.

In 1887 the U.S. government passed a law requiring tribes in Oklahoma to give each of their members 160 acres and to surrender what was left of their reservations to white settlers. The Osage fought this law, and it took almost 20 years for Congress to agree to their terms. In 1906 the tribe not only got the individual acreage increase to 657 acres, but the government agreed that white settlers could not get the leftover land. The Osage tribe also retained ownership of the mineral rights under all of their land. Each member of the tribe not only received their 657 acres but annually shared equally in the royalties from the oil taken out of the ground by the petroleum companies. With the oil boom of the 1920s, the Osage became the wealthiest Indian nation in the country. However, they continued to be preyed upon. During the 1920s a series of Osage murders were covered up with the help of dishonest government officials so that white men could gain control of oil royalties.

Many whites who met the Osage were fascinated by them. Washington Irving visited Independence, Missouri in 1832 and wrote to his sister that "the Osage were the finest looking Indians I have ever seen." They were described as over six feet tall. American painter George Catlin, who in 1832 spent time with the Osage painting them, wrote, "The Osage may justly be said to be the tallest race of men in North America. They are well-proportioned. Their movements graceful and quick." James Audubon, on his 1843 trip through this part of the country to paint the birds of North America, described them as "well formed, athletic and robust. Men of noble aspect."

Those Indians who took care of the land that became Kansas City understood what the white man was doing to their lives. Osage chief Le Soldat du Chene, who was one of the chiefs who signed the 1808 treaty that removed the tribe from the Place of Many Swans, had this to say after the tribe gave up their village:

"I see and admire your way of living, your good warm house, your extensive cornfields, your gardens. You whites possess the power of subduing almost every animal you see. You are surrounded by slaves.

Everything about you is in chains and you are slaves yourself. I fear if I should change my pursuit for yours, I, too, should become a slave."

Osage chief Le Soldat du Chene, whose French name means Soldier of the Oak, signed the 1808 Osage treaty.

BUYERS AND SELLERS

Trade was responsible for Kansas City's beginnings. The Indians did their share even before the white man came. Some tribes roamed the country bartering for goods that would be traded over and over again, which would explain both the arrowheads made of rocks and minerals from the Northeast and Southwest and the beads of ocean shells that archeologists have found at local Indian sites.

Coronado's records concerning his 1541 march through New Mexico mention an Indian Fair in the Taos pueblo. It was a yearly event attended by Indians from Mexico and New Mexico. By the 17th century members of other tribes, including Plains Indians, were making the trip to the fair. Then the Spanish, and later the French, seeing the Taos Fair as a profitable outlet for European merchandise, began attending. In spite of the Taos Indians driving the Spaniards out of their pueblo in 1680 (they returned in 1692), and the occasional Navajo, Comanche, and Apache raids and massacres perpetrated on those traveling to Taos, the fair survived. When it resumed the next year, the Indians would trade the loot and captives taken in the raids of the previous year.

By the middle of the 1700s, French traders from St. Louis began making the yearly trip to the New Mexican fair. They traveled up the Mississippi and Missouri Rivers in boats made of logs, loaded with merchandise, horses, and mules. They left the river somewhere in the vicinity of the confluence of the Missouri and Kaw, then proceeded overland through the plains and mountains to reach New Mexico. It wasn't an easy trip, but it must have been worth it. The Indians traded fur pelts, buffalo robes, and silver for guns, gun powder, cloth, and jewelry. The Spanish from South America and Mexico who attended the fair were also eager customers. They brought merchandise to exchange for French goods and returned south to re-trade or sell. The event was a money maker all around.

This fair created an appetite for trade goods among the Indians and Spanish that would lead later to the success of the Santa Fe Trail trade. New Mexico still hosts several annual Indian fairs or markets, the biggest of which is in Santa Fe. Today's Kansas Citians seem to have an affinity for New Mexico. Many area residents travel to the Indian fairs to buy and sell as people have for centuries.

The Kansa and Osage were known for their trapping and hunting ability. The French, and later American, traders would build trading forts and stations close by Indian villages. One of the reasons the French established Fort Cavaginal in 1744 near Leavenworth, Kansas, was to trade with the Kansa Indians for valuable fur pelts. Fort Osage, built by the U.S. government in 1808 near the relocated Osage village, became the largest of the so-called trading "factories." A piece of cloth or some ribbon or beads might be purchased for a beaver pelt. The steady stream of Indians bringing their furs to exchange for white men's merchandise made the fort a thriving business. The Indians became dependent on these goods, however, and this hastened their removal from their lands. The prosperity of the trade attracted more white men to the Missouri Valley who would want Indian land.

John Jacob Astor's American Fur Company had a monopoly on the fur trade in America. The Chouteau family in St. Louis, agents for the Astor company, joined other traders in pressuring the government to get out of the fur business. The success of the fort's fur trading ultimately brought Francois Chouteau to the area in 1821 to build a trading station that started Kansas City.

By the end of the 18th century, top hats and coats were made of fur, and coats with fur collars became high fashion in this country and in Europe. Furs were also used as blankets and seat coverings for carriages. Fur merchants saw the forests west of the Mississippi as a potential gold mine. The French were already in place and had the contacts to expand the market. The French themselves did not trap for furs; they located a supply and traded for them.

Francois' grandfather Auguste Chouteau, along with Pierre Laclede, founded St. Louis in 1764. Auguste was soon into the fur trading. He built Fort Carondelet near the Place of Many Swans in 1795 in order to trade with the Osage. Four generations of Chouteaus thrived in the fur trading business: Auguste's son Pierre Chouteau, his sons Francois, Frederick, and Cyprian, and their children all traded with the Indians for furs.

Francois was born into the wealthy family in 1792. It was said he was well-educated. In 1819 Francois married 18-year-old Berenice Menard, daughter of Pierre Menard, president of the French Legislative Council of the Illinois Territory. The newlyweds spent their honeymoon boating on the Missouri River, going as far as St. Joseph to make trading agreements with the Robidoux family there. They also looked for a likely spot to build a trading station near the confluence of the Kaw and Missouri Rivers.

After their return to St. Louis, Francois sent Louis Beretholet to build a cabin on the site he selected on his wedding trip. "Grand Louis," as he was called because of his enormous size, and his wife and three men came here in 1820. They cleared the land and cut down trees to build the Chouteaus' log cabin home. The cabin was constructed on the north bank of the Missouri River, east of today's Chouteau Bridge. It was near an old Indian trail that cut from the river north. With the Missouri River at his front door, Francois had access to the Kaw, the Platte, and other smaller rivers. The trail and the river offered him routes to many Indian villages in the region.

The cabin was almost finished when Sauk Indians destroyed it. Grand Louis rebuilt it. Sometime between the spring of 1821 and the next year, Francois, Berenice, and their infant son arrived with 35 men. The additional men came to build quarters on the opposite riverbank for the workers who would stay at the post as well as for visiting traders and trappers. The Osage called the settlement "Cho-To-To-Van"—Chouteau's Town—but the traders, trappers, adventurers, and various travelers who came there called it simply "The Camp." It was not only a trading post; it became a gathering place, especially during the winter months when the weather limited travel. This was the start of a community that would become Kansas City.

The word went out: the Chouteaus were buying and trading. Fur pelts were brought in by Indians and trappers from as far away as the Rocky Mountains. And Francois and his helpers traveled to Indian villages to get more. Furs were piled high on flat-keel boats and sent downriver to St. Louis. When the boats returned, they were full of merchandise to use in trading for the next batch of furs.

By 1825 the Chouteau family had grown. There were two new babies (Francois and Berenice would have nine sons and one daughter, but five sons would die very young), and Francois' two brothers, Cyprian and Federick, came to the post to help with the growing fur-trading business.

Contrary to popular belief, there was not just one Chouteau trading post; there was a chain of them. Cyprian built and operated one called "Four Houses" on the north side of the Kaw River near today's Bonner Springs. He named it thus because four houses were built connected to each other like a fort. (Sometimes this post was also referred to as "Four Corners.") In order to trade with the Shawnee, Delaware, and Kansa, the Chouteau brothers also built and operated posts near today's Turner, Topeka, Argentine, and Lawrence, all in Kansas. A post was also opened two miles from the Shawnee Mission, still standing in Johnson County. Cyprian married the daughter of a Shawnee chief and lived with that tribe. Frederick also spent considerable time living with the Kansa.

After the 1826 flood washed away the Randolph trading site, Francois salvaged what merchandise he could and moved his family to Four Houses. New quarters and a warehouse were constructed on the south bank of the Missouri River (near today's Troost Avenue) and he moved his family back. However, this Chouteau operation would become more of a distribution warehouse—receiving fur pelts from the other posts, sending them on to St. Louis, and receiving merchandise in return that would be distributed to the posts as trade for more furs.

While Francois and his workers traveled to the posts and Indian villages, the women were left to take care of the settlement. Madame Chouteau and Madame Beretholet both knew how to use guns. They killed bears and other wild animals that came into the post and would frighten off Indians who didn't seem friendly. Both of these ladies took care of those who became ill during the epidemics of cholera, smallpox, and other diseases that descended on the community. They nursed the Indians and slaves along with the white members of the settlement. Madame Chouteau brewed medicines from herbs, baptized all who were dying, and adopted the children who had lost their parents. It was said that she used her wedding gown to make shrouds for those who died. She also lost two of her own children in a cholera epidemic.

In 1838 Francois was in Indian territory to trade for a herd of wild horses. On his return trip home, he chose to ride one that appeared tame. Near the Flint Hills, a renegade group of Indians stampeded the horses, trying to steal some of them. In the confusion, the horse that Francois was riding threw him and the other horses trampled him to death. His sons Edmond, 17, and Pierre, 15, were with him but not harmed. They brought his body home and Berenice took him to St. Louis for burial. She later returned to the settlement, but Francois' brothers and sons took over the management of the warehouse.

By this time, the U.S. government was paying Indians annuities in silver to move off of their lands and relocate in Kansas Territory. Indians came through the settlement with silver to spend. Merchants opened general stores near Chouteau's warehouse to sell to the native people and increasing number of travelers moving west. Several warehouses were built on the levee to hold supplies. Only one was constructed of brick, and it would be the only building to survive the 1844 flood.

This Indian trade would also add to the cash drawers of merchants in West Port. John McCoy, an early settler in the levee town, was the founder of West Port. In 1832 he built a log cabin/general store at what is now the northeast corner of Westport Road and Pennsylvania. He surveyed the land around his store and filed a plat in 1833. There were already people living in the area, but McCoy was the first to make it legally a town and give it a name. His attempt to sell lots failed, so he offered to give land away free to anyone who would build in West Port. A harness maker and saddle maker took him up on the free lots, and so did a tavern owner. Soon there were 50 people in the town and several businesses along Westport Road. John Sutter opened a store there, but he wasn't a shopkeeper and the enterprise failed. Sutter moved west and got a land grant in California's Sacramento Valley. In building a mill on his property, workmen found the first nuggets of gold that started the 1849 California gold rush.

The Indians crossing over to the Kansas Territory stopped just beyond West Port to camp in a large orchard and near a spring. Later newspaper articles quoted early West Port residents who spoke about seeing hundreds of tepees and campfires in the apple orchard situated south of Westport Road, in an area now bordered by Southwest Trafficway and State Line Road.

There are events in every city's history that mark the change in its direction. The Santa Fe Trail trade did this for Kansas City. The trail started by mistake. In 1821 William Becknell left Franklin, Missouri, with pack mules carrying trade goods bound for Comanche territory. He lost his way when crossing the mountains through the Raton Pass. Mexican soldiers who found him told about the riches in Santa Fe and led him there. Becknell sold all of his merchandise in Santa Fe at such a profit that after he returned to Franklin, he convinced businessmen to back him in yearly trips with wagons full of trade goods. This venture became so successful that others began taking wagons to Santa Fe.

But Franklin was over 100 miles from the crossover to Kansas Territory. The animals were tired out before they began the trip west. When Independence, Missouri, was founded in 1827, it was closer to the west border of Missouri, so the Santa Fe trade origination point was shifted there. Supplies were dropped off at the Wayne City landing to the north of Independence. To avoid the Blue River, the wagon route from Independence traveled south along today's Blue Ridge Boulevard to about what would become 122nd Street, where a town called New Santa Fe was established. The wagons then moved west to cross the prairie.

The Mexican War interrupted the Santa Fe trade. But the traders and merchants at the riverfront and in West Port made money outfitting the soldiers at Fort Leavenworth as well as locals who joined military units to fight the war.

Starting in 1850, over 40,000 adventurers on their way to the goldfields of California or the silver mines of Colorado moved through the area. Many, needing supplies, stopped at both the levee town and West Port. John McCoy and the other West Port merchants needed their supplies quicker than Independence could deliver. McCoy got the steamboats to unload his merchandise at the natural rock levee landing at the end of Grand Avenue. What started as a convenience for John McCoy soon switched the origination point of the Santa Fe trade to the riverfront town. The wealth it attracted to both towns prompted more merchants to open stores. During the Santa Fe Trail trade, West Port, four miles to the south of the levee, would become better known than the Town of Kansas.

By the early 1850s, as many as five or six steamboats a day were unloading freight at the levee, just a narrow space barely wide enough for one wagon to pass another. Wagons lined up waiting to be loaded. Men—whites, black slaves, Mexicans, and halfbreeds—were also waiting to put the freight into the wagons so the oxen or mule teams could start on the long haul to Santa Fe.

The slow procession of wagons, from the first to the last, sometimes stretched three miles out from the levee. People living in the small town couldn't avoid the sights, sounds, and smells of the wagon train. The prairie schooners made noise clanking along. The men cursed and cracked whips across the backs of the straining animals. And the smells of so many animals and sweating men spread quite a distance.

To go south, the wagons went through a gully in the bluffs in back of the levee. This was the first main road called Market Street, now Grand Avenue. The wagons continued, passing east of the Public Square, today's City Market. The wagon trains made their way south to OK Creek, which ran west to east at about where Union Station is today. The creek often overflowed its banks, and the wagons had to adjust east or west to find a safer crossing. Once across the creek, the animals began the arduous pull uphill to 31st Street, where the trail leveled off. The wagons then turned west, cutting across the Penn Valley Park area, then turned south again toward West Port to cut across west to the Kansas Territory.

The wagon trains had to ford OK Creek in order to head south for the crossover into Kansas Territory on their way to Santa Fe.

The trail wasn't exact, as there were no real roads or streets then. The route might shift from side to side, depending on flooding conditions of OK Creek, tollgates put up by farmers (who wanted 50 cents a wagon), or the preference of the wagon master. After leaving West Port, the wagons would average 15 miles a day.

West Port had more than supply stores to attract the trade. The caravans' animals could feed to the west across the state line on the Shawnee Indians' unoccupied land. These grasslands also served as a rendezvous point for late wagons and a place the animals could rest after their long uphill climb. Returning from Santa Fe, wagon riders would stop here to spruce up before coming into town. Mexican traders coming from Sonora and Chihuahua carried large amounts of gold bullion and bars of silver aboard their wagons. These travelers found West Port a good place to spend their Spanish doubloons and Mexican pesos. The profits in trade attracted wagon, saddle, and bridle makers, food purveyors, clothing merchants, taverns, and everything that civilization had to offer. An article in an 1858 *Oregon Trails* newspaper stated, "Whiskey circulated more freely in West Port than is altogether safe in a place where every man carried a loaded pistol."

Two of the buildings constructed to serve those traveling on the trail still stand. The building on the northwest corner of Pennsylvania and Westport Road was built in 1851. Albert Boone, a grandson of Daniel Boone, had a store there. Slave auctions were held in the basement, and chains that held the slaves remain embedded in the walls there. The building just to the west was constructed in 1850 as a store and later purchased by James Bridger, Oregon Trail scout and an explorer of the West. Bridger built a house near 103rd and State Line by the Watts Mill, and he spent the remainder of his life there.

In 1902 the Wiedenmann family bought this building on the northwest corner of Pennsylvania and Westport Road and opened a grocery store. By the 1930s it was a bar. Since 1947 it has been Kelly's Westport Inn. The Wiedenmann family sold the building to the Kelly family in 1995.

Merchants made money and so did the freighters. Alexander Majors started his business by taking trade goods to Indian reservations. By 1854 he was involved in the Santa Fe trade, employing 1,200 men running 100 wagons and 12,000 oxen. He formed a partnership with William B. Waddell and William Russell. By 1858 the company had 120 wagon trains crossing the plains; each train consisted of 25 wagons, 3,600 men, and over 40,000 oxen. The company not only brought supplies to New Mexico, but supplied all of the military forts in the West. Their yearly gross exceeded $4 million in gold.

Majors and his partners started the Pony Express in 1860 to deliver mail from St. Joseph, Missouri, to Sacramento, California, in 10 days. Over 150 relay stations were built across 1,840 miles. Eighty riders were hired, mostly teenagers, as the weight of the man was a crucial factor in the speed of the horse. Each rider was given a shotgun and a Bible to take with him. Buffalo Bill Cody, age 15, was one of the riders, as was young James "Wild Bill" Hickok. Rider and horse endured for as far as they could, then stopped at a relay station where a fresh rider and horse would take the mail and gallop off. This exchange of men and horses continued as many times as needed to get to Sacramento. The expansion of the telegraph system across the country and the transcontinental railroad ended the Pony Express. Though it only lasted 18 months, the adventure still captures our imagination.

In 1856 Alexander Majors built a mansion at 83rd and State Line. This was the company's headquarters. Men, wagons, and hundreds of animals waited in the surrounding acreage to begin their journey west. The restored house has been designated as a Santa Fe Trail historic site and is open to the public.

Today, on the east side of Broadway at the intersection of Westport Road, is Pioneer Park, displaying statues of the three men who contributed to the early growth of the area: John McCoy, Alexander Majors, and Jim Bridger.

By 1857 there were over 300 merchants and freighters engaged in the Santa Fe trade in the two towns. In 1858 the Town of Kansas had $3 million in sales. The word was spreading about business opportunities, even back East. An article in a Boston newspaper stated, "The town is a place of considerable business and embraces all the elements of future greatness."

But the time of prosperity didn't last. By the fall of 1861, because of Kansas bushwhackers raiding wagon trains and the threat of the Civil War bringing military action to the Midwest, the Santa Fe trade ended. In fact, all business in both towns came to a standstill. There was no money coming in at all. Many people left to find a safer place to live. The Civil War was the death knell for West Port as a trading center. It never recovered. The town become a part of Kansas City in 1899 and lost its two-word name.

The fur trade lasted almost two centuries. Santa Fe Trail trade lasted only a brief four decades, but over the years has generated more books and newspaper stories. In 1987 the U.S. Congress approved a bill making the 950-mile Santa Fe Trail a national historic site. It was signed into law by President Ronald Reagan, who in his acting career had starred with Errol Flynn in the 1940 film, *The Santa Fe Trail.*

The end of the Santa Fe trade almost meant the end of the Town of Kansas. But after the Civil War, the building of a bridge just to the east of the levee, the first to span the Missouri, ushered in a new era of growth.

West Port's first City Hall, located at Broadway and Westport Road, was built in 1840. This photo shows the town's entire police force standing in front of the building. The officer on horseback is June Collins, a black policeman.

SETTLING IN

The Chouteaus have traditionally been credited as being the first white settlers in the Kansas City area, but it's actually a matter of defining "white" and "settler." There were certainly earlier settlers; some were not 100 percent white, and some only lived here for a time.

Daniel Morgan Boone, son of Daniel Boone, spent several winters living and trapping on the Blue River and Brush Creek at the end of the 18th century. Later he moved to Indian territory to live and work with several tribes. In 1831 Boone returned, purchased 80 acres near 63rd and Woodland, and started farming. He died of cholera in 1839 and was buried on his farm, where the grave remains to this day.

Shortly after the Louisiana Purchase, French Canadian trappers employed by the North American Fur Company settled in the West Bottoms on the Missouri side of the Kaw River. The area became known as "The French Bottoms." These men were part French and part Indian, and they had their Indian wives with them. They cleared the land, farmed, and set out traps along the Kaw. Their settlement was washed away by the 1844 flood.

The couple sent by the Chouteaus in 1820 to build their cabin should get the credit as the first white settlers. They lived here a whole year before Berenice and Francois arrived. But the Beretholets were Creoles, also half Indian and half French. Even though they remained in the settlement until they died, and Madame Beretholet was Berenice Chouteau's best friend, the couple has never received recognition as the area's first settlers.

Chouteau's second cabin built on the river's south bank after the 1826 flood sat on land that he had no right to. In fact, all of the French in the early settlement were squatters. Until the 1826 Osage treaty, the land belonged to the Indians. The government then offered the land for sale under the Homestead Rights Act. In early 1831 Gabriel Prudhomme, a French Canadian, paid $340 for a 257-acre tract of land stretching south from the river through a forest to Independence Avenue, west to Broadway, and east to Troost. This encompassed the French settlement and would make up all of the early Town of Kansas.

Prudhomme had plans. He was a blacksmith and was going to start a forge. He also planned to open a tavern and a store. However, sometime in the winter of 1831 he got into a barroom brawl with some fellow Canadians. When it was all over, Prudhomme lay dead and the murderer got away.

There was no will. The court appointed James Hyatt McGee as trustee for Prudhomme's wife and children. Five years later the oldest daughter married and petitioned the Jackson County Court to divide the land among her father's heirs. The court appointed a three-member commission to survey the land to assess its worth. They reported that the land was only valuable as a ferryboat landing. It was decided to sell the land and divide the sale money among the family members. On July 7, 1838, the land was put up for auction. Twenty-one bidders showed up, among them two of the commissioners who did the survey. The auctioneer, Mr. McGee, the family's trustee, sold the land quickly to a friend for $1,800. The other bidders protested that they had not had a chance to bid. The court put the sale aside and called for another auction in November.

Fourteen men organized The Town Company to bid for the land. They were all prominent merchants in Independence, West Port, and the riverfront town and had business or family ties to each other. The Town Company's bid for $4,220 was the highest received, and the Prudhommes were to be paid off in one year. However, several years passed and the Prudhommes received no money, so they sued The Town Company, who then sued them back as well as each other.

One of the company's members, John McCoy, who founded West Port, platted the land, paced off 86 lots, and offered them for sale. Only nine lots were sold. Later, in 1846, McCoy made a new plat, including some surrounding land that the group had purchased. Ninety-seven lots were sold for $22 to $341 each. Within a few years the lots that had been purchased for $30 sold for $7,000. Not bad for land that had been declared not worth very much!

The town needed a name. One member, Abraham Fonda, wanted to named the place "Port Fonda." Others suggested "Possumtrot." Finally they took the name of the Kansa Indians that lived across the river and called it the Town of Kansas. But the town was also referred to as "Kawsmouth," and steamboat captains called it "The Landing" or "West Port's Landing." To many it was "Chouteau's Town." The town's name would not become officially Kansas City until 1889.

In 1840 Father Nicholas Point made a map of the early settlement, showing the homes of the Catholics there. This is the earliest known map of the city. At the top of the rendering is the home of Mme. Gabriel (Susan) Prudhomme, whose husband had owned all of the land. You can see the "Grand Louis" house (#15) is right on the river near a stream

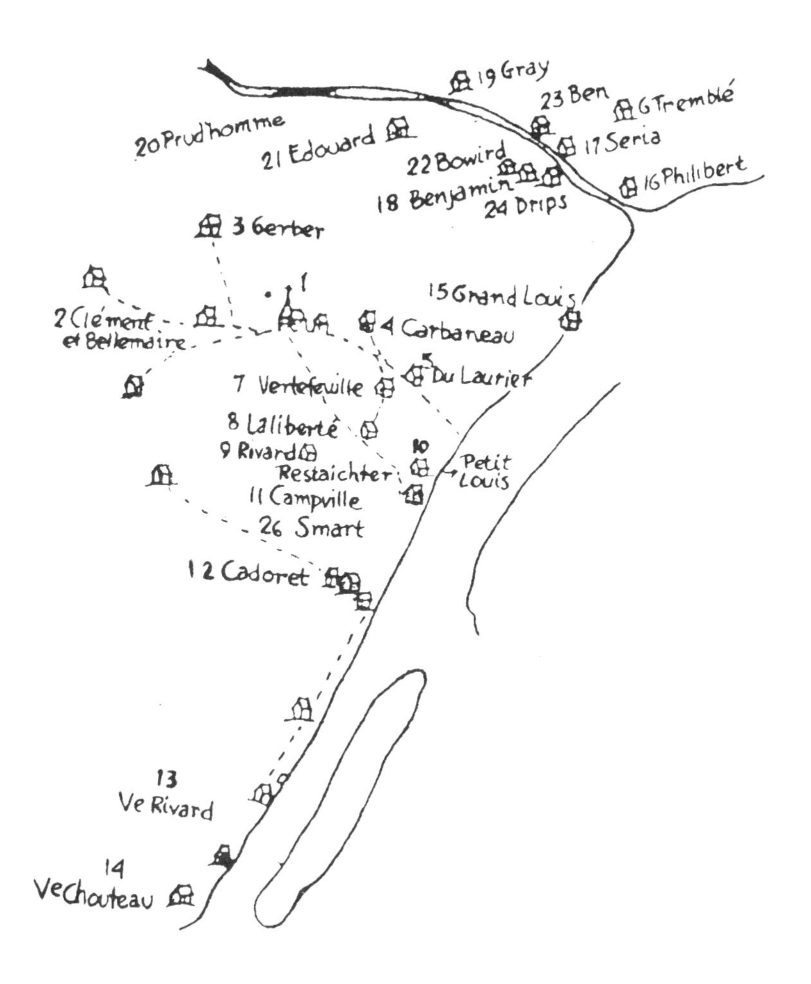

coming from Turkey Creek. His stepson, referred to as "Petit Louis," is east of him. Numbers 11 and 26 indicate two stores located on the riverfront. At the bottom of the map, number 14, is the house of Berenice Chouteau at Second and Cherry. When the 1844 flood hit the community, all of these homes, so close to the Missouri River, were swept away by the water. Mme. Chouteau had to be carried from her home. The French never rebuilt the settlement.

The city's first real hotel was built in 1849 by Dr. Benoist Troost and William Gillis, two of the town's leading citizens. This four-story, 60-room brick structure sat right on the edge of the river between Wyandotte and Delaware Streets. At different times it was called the Troost Hotel, the Gillis House, and the American Hotel.

The hotel's 8-by-10-foot rooms had space for a bed and little else. Sarah Coates, who arrived in town with her husband Kersey in 1856, was the first woman to stay in the hotel. She later told her daughter that after traveling on steamboats for almost 18 days, any kind of a resting place would be welcome. However, the dismal look of the hotel prompted her to cry, "Is this to be my home?"

A large bell on the roof was rung three times a day to call guests and townspeople to meals. It wasn't elegant dining, but in those early days the hotel was the only place to eat in town. Sixty people could dine at one time on the large tables in the hotel's lobby.

In the years 1856 to 1857, over 27,000 guests from all over the world signed the hotel's register. After the Civil War, though, better hotels were built south of the levee. There were several fires at the Gillis Hotel and it fell on bad times. Before it was demolished in 1909, the place was used as a pickle factory.

Until the late 1850s, almost everything that was Kansas City was concentrated between the river and the Third Street bluffs, some which were 100 feet high. The levee's wealthy merchants built fine homes of brick and walnut on the top of these bluffs to take advantage of the river view. It was the city's first wealthy neighborhood. Pearl Street from Grand to Walnut was the bluff's main thoroughfare.

These merchants may have made their money on sound business deals, but they built their homes on unstable ground. Every time there was heavy rain, mud slides threatened their homes. Thousands of years of erosion had cut three natural ravines through the bluffs. The first wagons leaving the levee to go to West Port to begin their journey to Santa Fe used the widest ravine, called Market Street. To accommodate more wagon traffic, men with shovels made Market wider. Later, using old-fashioned gunpowder, the other ravines were blasted open so they, too, could be used as roads. The bluffs became unstable, and the houses on Pearl Street began to slide into the gullies below. In the late 1890s what was left of Pearl Street was called Hobo Hill because tramps had made a camp there.

After the Civil War some of the Pearl Street residents, still wanting a river view, settled on the bluffs above the Kaw River. A small log cabin church had been built there in 1835. Father Benedict Roux, who was pastor of the Chouteau settlement, in 1834 spent $6.00 of his own money to buy a 40-acre plot of land near 11th and Broadway. Some of the

At left is a house perched on the Pearl Street bluffs at Third and Walnut Streets in 1868.

land was sold off but 10 acres were kept on which to build the church. This land is still owned by the Catholic diocese.

Before the church could be built, Father Roux left town, but Berenice Chouteau saw to the construction. Though called St. Francis Regis, it was known as Chouteau's church. In 1857 a larger brick church was built on the site by Father Bernard Donnelley, who was appointed pastor of the Town of Kansas that year. The priest arranged for 300 Irish laborers, all from Ireland's Connaught province, to come to town to erect his church. He even had quarters built for them. A parish brickyard supplied the bricks for the church, located next to the city's Catholic burial ground. When the job was done, many Irishmen stayed in the town and became the laborers and craftsmen who built the city's early structures. The Cathedral of the Immaculate Conception, now on the southwest corner of 11th and Broadway, was constructed in 1882, replacing Donnelley's church.

The first home built on the west bluffs was a log cabin constructed in 1838 by Andrew Drips, an Indian trader. In 1857 his son-in-law, William Mulkey, also an Indian trader, built a large house he called his Western Palace on the southern part of the bluffs. For its construction Mulkey imported bricks from St. Louis, white pine from Pittsburgh, and red walnut from California. The house sat high enough that the porches on three sides gave a view not only of the Kaw but also the Missouri River. Mulkey's friend, the legendary frontiersman Kit Carson, was often a guest there.

Kersey Coates bought land on the west bluffs from Berenice Chouteau and built his home there in 1859. Coates, a major force in the growth of the Town of Kansas, saw the bluffs as a potential exclusive residential neighborhood, similar to those in his hometown of Philadelphia, Pennsylvania. He even named the street in front of his house Pennsylvania Avenue. Later, Coates would build the Coates Opera House and develop a hotel just to the east of his home. After the Civil War, some veterans who had been officers in the Union Army started building large homes on these bluffs. Those who fought on the side of the Confederacy called these wealthy Republicans "Silk Stockings" and dubbed the area "Silk Stocking Ridge." The Southern sympathizers also called the neighborhood "Quality Hill." Meant to be derogatory, this name stuck.

By the 1890s, many bluff residents, attracted to the exclusive new neighborhoods being developed and wanting to escape from the smells coming up from the stockyards, moved south. Their abandoned mansions became hospitals, churches, apartments, and rooming houses. Workingmen also built some smaller houses to the east of the bluffs, and from 1900 to 1920 several apartment houses went up in the area for those who worked downtown. The 1950s saw several upscale apartments constructed on the north end of Jefferson Street that gave residents an overview of the confluence of the two rivers. Most of what was left of the old mansions and even the smaller houses were demolished in the 1980s to make way for new apartments and town houses. These were designed to fit in with the few historic structures still remaining. Over 150 years after it was first settled, today many Kansas Citians enjoy living on Quality Hill.

Cutting into the Third Street bluffs not only made way for wagons going to Santa Fe but pushed the riverfront town south away from the levee. Soon the town's center was the Public Square, a block of land bounded by Main, Walnut, Fourth, and Fifth Streets. The land was donated by the Gillis family in 1846 to be used as a public square forever by the citizens of the town. The spring in the Square was the only source of clear water for those who lived nearby.

After the Civil War, people also started moving east and south away from the Public Square area. Homes first went up along east Eighth and Ninth and their adjacent streets. By 1885, grand houses were being built along Independence Avenue and then north along Gladstone and Benton Boulevards. Until after the turn of the century, this would be home to some of the city's most prominent people. That era of the town's social life revolved around Independence Avenue and Quality Hill.

Independence Avenue is the city's oldest east-west thoroughfare. In the 1830s, people from Independence, Missouri, used the road to get to the riverfront town. It was listed as Independence Avenue in the first city directory printed in 1860. Through the efforts of one of the street's best-known residents, August R. Meyer (called the "father" of Kansas City's park system), Independence Avenue from Woodland to Gladstone was designated in 1895 as the city's first boulevard.

Judge Churchill White's mansion was on Independence Boulevard just east of Maple Street.

Those building these mansions were presidents of banks and owners of large stores, as well as prominent physicians, lawyers, and civic leaders. It was said that these newly rich citizens moved to Independence Avenue because they resented the "northern snootiness" of the aristocratic pioneer families who had settled on Quality Hill. There are still remnants of the early mansions along Gladstone and Benton Boulevards, but none of the grand houses still stand along Independence Boulevard.

It is all very well for a town to boast of exclusive residential districts, but Kansas City's growth depended on vast numbers of people who worked hard for a living and paid taxes. Industrial districts were developing below the northeast bluffs and east in the Blue Valley. And the surrounding area offered affordable land where small workmen's houses could be built. By 1893, electric trolleys were running on Independence Avenue and St. John Avenue, providing cheap transportation to jobs.

The Blue Valley industrial district starts at the eastern end of Independence Avenue, and this is where the Kansas City Bolt and Nut Company was established in 1887. The factory would grow into Sheffield Steel, one of the nation's top steel producers. (Today it is Armco Steel.) The Ford Motor Company located a factory in Blue Valley in 1909. The Montgomery Ward Company moved there in 1913, building a large distribution warehouse just north of Independence Avenue at St. John and Belmont. In 1918, The Kansas City Street Railway erected car barns and shops on Brighton six blocks north of Independence Avenue. In the train yards below the Northeast bluffs, there were switching yards and a large train repair roundhouse. All of these enterprises created thousands of jobs, and hundreds of small houses sprang up in the Northeast and East sections for homes for their workers.

By the 1890s, the wealthy were moving south. When the *New York Herald* published a list of 23 millionaires living in Kansas City in 1901, a fourth of them lived on "Millionaire's Row," a section of Troost from 26th to 27th Streets. William J. Smith, who developed the city's first cable car system, built a home at 3000 Troost that was typical of the mansions there. It cost $110,000 in 1890! Each room was panelled in a different fine wood and throughout the house were massive fireplaces with mantles of onyx and marble. Smith's library contained over 2,000 volumes, said to be the finest in the city. There was a smoking room, a billiard room, and a ping-pong room. The third floor held two ballrooms where a full orchestra provided music for weekly dances. Smith's house

The Janssen Place gate still identifies the Hyde Park neighborhood.

was the first in town to be wired for electricity and the first to have a water-cooled air conditioning system. Unfortunately, no evidence remains today of "Millionaire's Row."

By the turn of the century, some of those who had built mansions on Independence Boulevard and Troost were moving to Hyde Park, then defined as stretching between McGee and Oak, from 36th to 38th streets. Those who had lived on main streets liked the fact that the natural topography of Hyde Park had been left undisturbed. A part of a private park in the neighborhood was turned into the Hyde Park Country Club. This club was located at the south end of the neighborhood, and the land is now a part of Kansas City's Parks Department.

Janssen Place became the most exclusive address in Hyde Park. Built by men who had made their money in the lumber business, the street was sometimes called "Lumberman's Row." This private area could only be accessed through an ornate stone gate on 36th Street.

While the mansions along Independence Boulevard are gone, many of the Hyde Park houses built at the turn of the 20th century have been maintained. The area is still a desirable address.

In the 1890s William Rockhill Nelson, publisher of *The Kansas City Star,* started buying land south of Hyde Park, east to Harrison and from 43rd south to Brush Creek. He built his own home there and created the Rockhill district, filled with homes of individual design that were constructed with the area's limestone and the finest lumber. The houses were not side by side but situated on lots that allowed plenty of light into their interiors. In 1900 Nelson paid to have Rockhill Road built through his district, allowing for a trolley line next to his road. At the southern end of his road, he put in a limestone bridge across Brush Creek.

Jessie Clyde Nichols admired the detail and care that Nelson took with his Rockhill neighborhood. Nichols' first housing development was in Kansas City, Kansas. Then in 1905, he bought 10 acres at 50th and Grand, just east of the Kansas City Country Club golf course. He built houses on the property and they sold. By 1909 his company had an agreement with the heirs to the Seth Ward farm to develop over 1,000 acres surrounding the golf club, south of Brush Creek from Main to Ward Parkway.

Nichols knew that those who were making money in the city's fast-growing economy would appreciate homes not too far from downtown. And being able to live close to the golf course at 51st and Wornall Road would be an added attraction. Nichols took the club's name for his neighborhood, and it became the Country Club district.

Like William Rockhill Nelson, J.C. Nichols believed that streets should follow the natural contours of the land. Plantings of shrubs and trees and the placement of statuary added to the beauty of the Country Club district. As one of the early planned residential developments, it became a model for urban planning all across the country.

Nichols encouraged Seth Ward's sons, Hugh and John, to give 90 acres of land west of the district to the city for the construction of a sweeping roadway. Ward Parkway, leading south from The Plaza, was landscaped with gardens, trees, ponds, and sculptures, and it is still regarded as one of America's great thoroughfares.

The majority of the population had no choice as to where they lived. The poor, immigrants and blacks, lived wherever they could afford to, often sharing the same slums. They did work that others didn't want to do because it was too strenuous, too dirty, or paid too little. The men were lucky if they got a day of working with a pick or a shovel on city improvements. Some of the women worked in the sweat shops of the early garment industry located on Broadway that paid by the piece completed.

Immigrants tended to cluster where their neighbors spoke their language, the grocery stores sold the kind of food they ate in the old country, and their churches were nearby. Neighborhoods in the city that identified with certain nationalities were plentiful until after the Second World War. When the immigrants' sons came back from the war, they wanted new houses and started moving to different parts of the city. However, there are still neighborhoods in Kansas City that can be identified by the people who live there.

The Columbus Park area, just east of the City Market, at one time was called "Little Italy" and sometimes "The North End." The area was the stopping-off place for most of the early immigrants who arrived by boat or at the train depot at Second and Wyandotte. Some Italians settled in that area in the 1870s, but the majority of residents, mostly from Sicily, arrived after the First World War.

Blacks and immigrants of all nationalities lived near the Market in tenements, sometimes cramming whole families into one room. They got along because they had poverty in common. When some of them attained financial stability and moved on to rent homes in better neighborhoods, their space filled with new immigrants. But the Italians stayed in that area the longest and it is still regarded as the Italian center of town, even though few live there now.

Meat-packing plants throughout the country sent representatives to East Europe to hire workers for their plants, thus bringing Serbians, Greeks, Russians, Slovakians, and Croatians to the West Bottoms stockyards to work. Many settled near their work in a place called "The Patch." Their houses were really only huts made of whatever materials were available. When they saved enough money to move on, many of them settled in the eastern part of Kansas City, Kansas. Today's residents of Strawberry Hill who are their descendents make sure that the area's ethnic identity is retained by festivals, offering the food, music, and dance of their ancestors.

At the turn of the century, when the American Radiator Company moved from Buffalo, New York, to the Blue Valley industrial district to take advantage of the steel production there, the company brought along several hundred Polish workers who were skilled in iron moulding. The workers built homes nearby in the area south of Truman Road by the Sheffield Steel plant, and their church had a Polish-speaking priest. Some of the descendents of these workers still live there and shop at a 75-year-old neighborhood Polish grocery store.

Mexican traders came to the Town of Kansas and West Port with the Santa Fe Trail wagons in the 1850s, and some kept permanent homes here. One wealthy merchant had a house near Wornall Road. In 1905 the Santa Fe Railroad brought a number of laborers from Mexico to work in the West Bottom train yards, housing them in boxcars in the Argentine section of Kansas City, Kansas. Those who stayed brought their families to live in overcrowded tenements or in old houses west of Summit Street from 23rd to 31st Streets.

In the early 1880s this area was an Irish community. So many lived there that the neighborhood was called "Irish Hill," even though Scandinavians, Germans, and other nationalities had homes there, too. Although there were many small houses lining the streets, some of the more well-to-do Irish built imposing brick homes in the area. A block of these houses on Jefferson Street between 17th and 18th still remain. By the beginning of the 20th century the Irish started to locate in the Northeast and Midtown. As the Irish moved out, the Mexicans moved in.

The chaos of the 1910 Mexican Revolution brought the first large numbers of Mexican immigrants to the area. Continuing poverty and oppression in Mexico drove another movement of immigrants to the area after 1920. Several early churches were established to serve the growing population. It was estimated that by 1940 over 5,000 Mexican Americans lived on the West Side.

The Guadalupe Center came about because of Dorothy Gallagher, a teacher, and other women who worked with the children on the West Side. Because of their concerns for the little ones' welfare, they established a center offering the Mexican immigrants health clinics, recreational activities, and social services. In 1932 Dorothy Gallagher's family purchased property at 23rd and Jarboe and built a Spanish Colonial-style building to house the center.

An energetic Mexican-American commercial district thrives on Southwest Boulevard, west from Broadway. Even though descendents of those early immigrants live all across the Metropolitan area, the West Side is still regarded as the heart of their community.

Blacks came here as slaves in the 1830s. In 1860 there were 4,000 slaves in Jackson County, the property of 898 owners. Slave auctions took place in Independence and also in West Port. After the Civil War there was an exodus of Southern blacks moving north to look for a better life. Some settled in the Town of Kansas. Like the immigrants, blacks earned low wages working in meat-packing plants, digging ditches for construction, laboring in train yards, and maintaining city streets. By the 1890s blacks made up 10 percent of the city's population. They lived in several slum areas including Hick's Hollow, which ran south of Independence Avenue from 12th to 19th Streets.

By the turn of the century those blacks who had prospered moved to Church Hill between Troost and Charlotte at 10th Street, where several churches were located. The blacks who were not well-to-do lived in an area called "The Bowery," from Troost east to Woodland, and from 17th to 20th.

Just after the First World War, Kansas City's black population had a shopping and cultural district in the area surrounding 18th and Vine that flourished for over 40 years. The black-owned hotels, restaurants, theaters, and businesses there gave their community pride and identity. The black population continued to expand to 28th Street, which became the dividing line between the black and white population until the 1950s, when blacks then started moving out of their traditional neighborhoods into other parts of the city.

By 1909 the southern city limit was 77th Street. Those who purchased land for development and those who were the first to build their houses in new areas pushed Kansas City's boundaries before them. Services such as water, gas, and, later, electricity were installed because wealthy residents demanded them. Electric street car companies extended their routes to connect the areas with downtown and other parts of the city.

Transportation and public utilities attracted others of humbler means to move around the fringes of the wealthier neighborhoods. And this was how the city grew.

TURKEY RED WHEAT AND TEXAS CATTLE

Indians were growing grain here long before white farmers came to the area. Early settlers bartered with them for wheat and other seeds. By the early 1830s there were enough farmers in Jackson County raising grain that the Fitzhugh brothers started a mill on Indian Creek just east of 103rd and State Line.

Water rushing through the creek pushed a paddlewheel that moved the mill's large grinding stones, thus when the creek froze or ran dry, the mill couldn't operate. After the fall harvest droves of farmers would come to the mill with wagons loaded, and the grinding took several days. The farmers brought their families with them and camped near the mill. This was a time to socialize after the hard work of the harvest. Farm wives, who seldom had a chance to talk to other women, visited and exchanged gossip. Children played games and fished in the creek. The men swapped stories and argued politics. There always seemed to be a fiddler in the group to play for nightly dancing by the campfires. Many young folk met their future spouses at the mill. The campgrounds surrounding the mill turned into a small town, named Dallas, later annexed into Kansas City, Missouri.

Drivers of cars traveling on State Line near 103rd Street may not realize that for over 100 years a grain mill operated nearby.

Anthony Watts purchased the mill in 1852. The operation was kept busy with local farmers and also by settlers crossing through the area who needed flour for the long trip. With his wife Sally, the daughter of Daniel Boone, Watts had 11 children. When he died in 1861, his son Stubbins took over, and then in turn each Watts generation assumed the responsibility of running the mill. It continued to operate until 1942. Today a portion of the land where Watts Mill was located belongs to the Kansas City Parks Department.

There also were other early mills in the area. One was located on the Little Blue River in 1844, another operated in Independence, and a Mr. Hickman ran a mill in what is now Hickman Mills in the southeastern part of Kansas City. There was also an early mill located where today the New York Life building stands at Ninth and Baltimore. A mill in West Port was powered by Mill Creek. The flour produced by these mills was not only for farmers but also was sold to levee and West Port merchants.

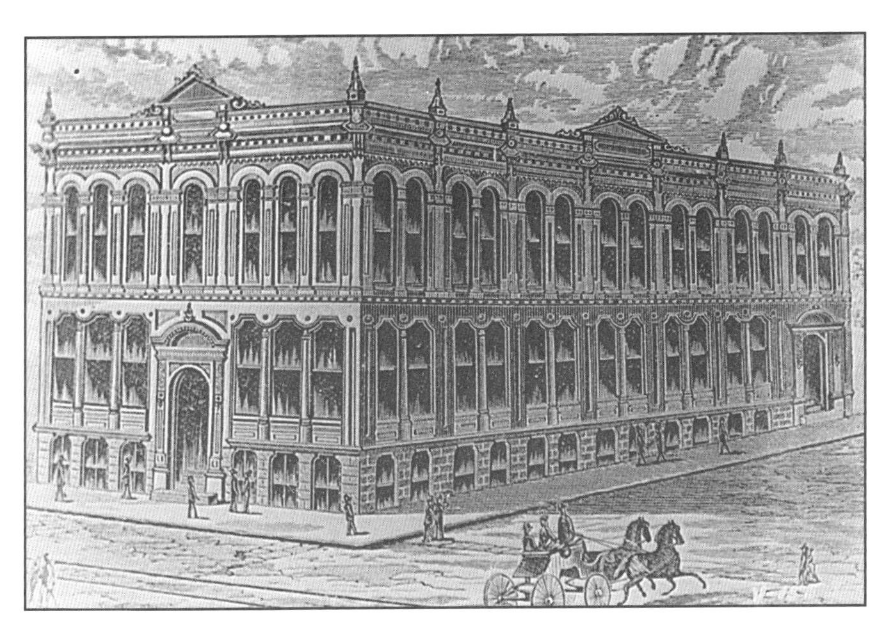

When this Board of Trade building was constructed in 1877, it was situated in the heart of town—at Fifth and Delaware.

A Kansas City Board of Trade was organized in 1856, though not exclusively for the grain business. A handful of levee merchants decided that they needed an association that would promote businesses in the town. A year later the group changed its name to The Commercial

Club, which later became The Chamber of Commerce.

By 1869 there was enough corn grown locally that corn buyers started another Board of Trade to set up guidelines for the inspection, buying, and selling of that crop. Later, wheat buyers joined. The Board was located in the West Bottoms across from Union Depot. When the new Armour Bank building on the southwest corner of Fifth and Delaware was finished in 1877, the Board of Trade moved in above the bank. The building, still there, was renovated into loft apartments in the early 1990s.

By 1878 the Board of Trade was dealing in nine million bushels of wheat annually. The wheat, not sold to local residents, was shipped out of the city on trains moving over the Hannibal Bridge. The expansion of railroad tracks across the country and events in other parts of the world had a profound impact on the emerging wheat industry here. A wheat seed brought from Russia not only helped to make the Midwest the bread basket of the world, but made Kansas City's Board of Trade the leader in marketing hard winter wheat.

The story of the seed that changed wheat growing starts with those who brought it to America. After being persecuted in several European countries, a large group of Mennonites (a Protestant sect) moved to Russia, settling in Crimea in the early 1700s. Catherine the Great, Czarina of Russia, promised they would have freedom of religion and would not be pressed into military service for 100 years.

Crimea once belonged to Turkey, and many Turkish farmers still owned farms there. The Mennonites saw that their farms produced a healthy crop of winter wheat in spite of droughts and insects. During that first fall, the new arrivals planted some of the wheat seeds given to them by the Turks. They were amazed at the hardy crop they grew that year. Over the next few years they bred those plants with other wheat varieties and produced an even better and more hardy wheat seed. They called it "Turkey Red."

Mennonite fields produced such record yields that the Turkish farmers asked for and were given the new seeds. In a few years all of the farms in Crimea were growing the special wheat. Mennonite settlements expanded and flourished. The settlers felt concern, however, that when Queen Catherine died, her successor might not honor her commitment to Mennonite religious freedom and exemption from conscription into the Russian army.

During this time, American railroads started a program seeking immigrants to settle along their tracks. The U.S. government had given railroad companies over a billion and a half acres of right of way to lay down tracks across the middle of the country for the transcontinental railroad connection. The excess land that the railroads didn't use was theirs to sell. They not only could make money from the sale of land, but also by settling people along their tracks — towns would develop and revenues would be generated by freight and passenger customers.

Soon after the Civil War, various railroad companies sent representatives throughout Europe to hand out pamphlets and put up posters telling of the excellent farming conditions in America. They not only described cheap fertile land in the central part of the country, but promoted America as a place of religious and political freedom. And the immigrants who bought land in the Midwest from the railroads were promised special reduced boat fares and low-priced train tickets.

When railroad representatives came to Russia in 1870 and talked about America's Midwest farmlands, the Mennonites listened. They felt it was time to leave Russia, so their leaders decided to send four young men to America to look for farmland. The men visited several Midwest states and returned to report that the land and climate in Central Kansas was much like that in Crimea. It would be a good place to grow their wheat.

The first group of Mennonite families, carrying Turkey Red wheat seed in burlap bags, began their long trip to America in 1873. They settled near Newton, Kansas, paying for their farmland in gold. First they built their houses and then in the fall they planted their winter wheat. When their first wheat was harvested in the spring, they knew that Kansas had been the right choice.

Other farmers in the area, who traditionally planted their wheat in the spring for late summer harvest, lost most of their crop to hailstorms and the rest to a plague of grasshoppers. The only farmers whose crop hadn't suffered were the Mennonites, who had harvested their wheat before the hail and insect season. They shared their seeds with the other farmers who planted them that fall and reaped large wheat crops the next spring. One by one entire villages left Russia for Kansas, and eventually almost 9,000 Mennonites would settle there.

It took several years for farmers across Kansas to hear about the wonders of Turkey Red, but by 1919 the hardy crop was grown not only throughout Kansas but in Nebraska, Oklahoma, and Colorado as well. Today most of America's wheat export is the Turkey Red winter variety.

Although the seeds have been interbred with other wheats over the years, seeds planted today can be traced back to those brought by Mennonites from Russia in burlap bags.

The large wheat harvests in Kansas not only pushed Kansas City's Board of Trade into national recognition in the grain cash and futures market, but prompted the building of grain elevators and milling operations in the East and West Bottoms. The Board of Trade soon outgrew its headquarters on Delaware. In 1887 the Exchange Building was constructed for them on the northeast corner of Eighth and Wyandotte.

With the opening of Union Station bringing more trains into the city, wheat was freighted to all parts of the nation as well as to shipping ports that sent it overseas.

The increased grain transactions spurred the growth of the Board of Trade. Needing a larger trading floor and room for more traders offices, in 1926 the Board moved into a 14-story building in the city's investment center on the northeast corner of 10th and Wyandotte. And the institution has continued to outgrow its quarters over the years. In 1964, not quite 100 years after its founding, the Kansas City Board of Trade moved south, constructing a building just beyond the Country Club Plaza at 49th and Main Streets.

Mennonites, farmers, merchants, and traders contributed to make Kansas City a leader in the grain industry. Today the Kansas City Board of Trade is the second largest grain exchange in the country. The city stands second in wheat flour production and third in grain elevator storage capacity.

The Board of Trade has survived as one of the city's major business institutions. The Kansas City Stockyards, also founded in the middle of the 19th century and once the second largest meat industry in the country, is no more.

Even before the Texas cattle drives brought large numbers of cows and steers to the West Bottoms, there was hoof stock here—the oxen that pulled settlers' wagons overland to the area. Some of these work animals were slaughtered for their meat. When the origination point for the Santa Fe Trail was switched to the levee town, thousands of oxen were pastured in areas around West Port and near the Alexander Majors home. The two early towns had no problem putting beef on the table.

Before the Civil War, some cattle were driven north from Texas to Sedalia, Missouri, to be shipped east by a train connection there. But the war stopped the Texas cattle drives. In 1866 Jessie Chisholm and his partner James Mead traveled from Texas through what is now Oklahoma on an old Indian trail headed for a trading post near a Wichita Indian village. They brought trade goods and 250 head of Texas cattle. Mead went on to found the city of Wichita. The trail, named after Chisholm, would become the route that carried millions of cattle to the stockyards in Kansas City's West Bottoms. The heavy traffic of the cattle pounded the dirt so solid that it created a channel 200 yards wide through the plains.

It was estimated that by the end of the Civil War more than five million head of cattle were waiting in Texas to be sold. There was also a meat shortage in the Northern states. Joseph G. McCoy, called "The Father of Kansas City's Cattle Industry," put supply and demand together by connecting Chisholm's trail to rail connections in Kansas so that cattle could be delivered to the West Bottom stockyards.

McCoy had been a cattle buyer in Illinois, where he paid as much as $100 a head. The Texas variety, however, was going at $2 to $3 a head. At that price, McCoy knew that if he could get the cattle to the West Bottoms where it would be convenient for buyers, the stock would sell cheap and big profits could be made. There was a Kansas Pacific Railroad track across the middle of Kansas that brought trains into the State Line Depot in the West Bottoms. McCoy's idea was to mark the old Chisholm Trail from Wichita to this track so that the animals could be herded to the trains, then loaded into cattle cars and delivered to the stockyards.

To bankroll the project, McCoy approached three railroads that would benefit from shipping cattle. The Missouri Pacific doubted that he could pull it off. The Kansas Pacific only offered McCoy a cut rate on shipping charges. But the Hannibal Railroad, at that time building the first bridge across the Missouri, realized the potential and gave him financial backing. McCoy bought land at a dollar an acre near the Kansas Pacific track and built cattle pens for 3,000 head. He also constructed a loading chute, erected a barn to hold 120 horses, and built a three-story hotel for the cowhands—all in 60 days. McCoy hired men to mark the trail from Wichita with little mounds of earth to guide the drovers. Then he sent others throughout Texas to post notices telling ranchers that if they drove their herds to the railroad track in Kansas, the stock could be shipped to the West Bottoms where buyers were waiting. To attract cattle buyers, McCoy ran full-page advertisements in newspapers throughout the Midwest. The ads said that Texas cattle could be purchased in the

West Bottoms at low prices, guaranteeing profits.

The first Texas cattle drive arrived in 1867. That year, 35,000 head were loaded onto trains and brought into the West Bottoms, where they sold quickly as predicted. The next year, cowboys moved herds of 1,000 to 3,000 at a time from Wichita to the train tracks. This trail became known as McCoy's Trail.

Cowhands were paid off when they reached the tracks, where soon there were saloons, dance halls, and other amusements. Many cowboys stayed in the area and spent their money. This was the start of Abilene, Kansas. It was a rough town, and later Wild Bill Hickok was hired as town marshal to keep order.

Some cowhands rode the train to the stockyards. They found plenty of places to spend their wages in the Town of Kansas, where opposite the Market Square were dozens of saloons, gambling halls, and brothels that beckoned for their money.

There were other cattle trails leading to other cities with rail connections, but because the Kansas City stockyards were the closest to the southwest cattle lands and rail connections were in place early, the stockyards here became second only to Chicago in the meat industry.

The Kansas City Stockyards Company was incorporated in 1871 on a 13 - 1/2 acre plot of land in the Bottoms at 12th and State Line, near the Kansas Pacific train tracks. That year, the first small Livestock Exchange Building was constructed. The company didn't realize that the cattle business would accelerate so quickly. The next year the building doubled in size to handle the business generated by the thousands of cattle, hogs, sheep, and mules that the trains kept bringing into the stockyards. So much cash was changing hands between buyers and sellers that two banks eventually opened in the Livestock building.

The cattle business outgrew the headquarters again. In 1876 a three-story Livestock Exchange building was constructed at 16th and State Line. Even though the structure was remodeled several times, livestock trading grew to such an extent that more space was needed. At the turn of the century the stockyards company drew up plans for a building that would have enough room to handle future cattle business. The nine-story Livestock Exchange Building at 1600 Genessee Street, with space for 475 offices, was completed in 1911 and it's still there.

The first meat-processing plant was not in the West Bottoms but on the levee, just east of Grand Avenue. It opened in 1859 and operated until the Civil War. By the time the first Texas cattle arrived, there were

The first Livestock Exchange was enlarged several times. Two banks were put into the building because too much cash was being carried around by cattle buyers and sellers.

several small packinghouses in the West Bottoms ready to process meat. In 1871 Plankington & Armour (later Armour & Company) built a plant near the stockyards, where they soon employed 600 workers. Over the next 15 years, nine major meat-packing companies opened plants in the West Bottoms, including Swift & Co., Cudahy Packing Company, and Wilson & Co. Eventually these plants employed thousands, and their payrolls soon reached $6 million annually.

Railroads extending into Texas ended the cattle drives in 1881. Their demise was inevitable. There were tracks close to most cattle towns, the trains brought the cattle directly to the stockyards, and because the cattle were not herded overland, they didn't lose weight and thus sold for more.

The American Royal grew out of stock shows and agricultural fairs, the first of which was held in 1871. Schools were closed and most of the businesses in town shut down so that everyone could go on opening day. The fair attracted visitors from all over the Midwest. Special trains brought people from surrounding states, and Indians traveled from their reservations.

A parade proceeded from the levee to the fairgrounds at the McGee farm, near 15th and Campbell. *The Kansas City Times* reported that 20,000 people (more than half the city's population) turned out to look at the farm implements, machinery, and horticultural exhibits.

The fair offered culture along with agriculture. A Fine Art Hall managed by noted painter George Caleb Bingham exhibited not only several of his paintings but also reproductions of masterpieces. However, *The Times* reflected the fair's homespun atmosphere when it reported that "a huge porker escaped from a pig pen and on his escape route ran under a lady and carried her a distance of 15 or 20 feet."

That first fair was so popular that it was repeated the next year on 97 acres of land near the McGee farm. A 20,000-seat grandstand was built for viewing farm animal competitions. There also was an unplanned event at that 1872 fair. Robbers, reported to be Jesse James and his gang, held up the ticket booth and grabbed the cash box that contained $978. The ticket seller fought with one of the robbers, who shot at him. The bullet hit a little girl standing nearby. She was not seriously wounded, and the robbers got away.

The fairs continued to be popular. Harness racing was included in 1874. After a fire destroyed the grandstand and main hall in 1881, the fair was moved to West Port near Southwest Trafficway and Valentine Road. In 1887 the fair returned to the east side of town as the opening event for the new Crystal Palace built at 13th and Agnes.

Modeled after London's famous building of the same name, the Palace offered 17 acres of floor exhibit space under an 80,000 square-foot glass, domed roof. President Grover Cleveland opened the fair that year, which included not only agricultural exhibits from the United States but also from Guatemala, Venezuela, and Columbia. Thousands came, many to see the new building. The fairs continued to be popular year after year, but the Crystal Palace didn't last—Midwest hailstorms knocked out all the glass. Abandoned in 1893, the decaying building was eventually destroyed by fire in 1903.

Cattle shows in the stockyards can be traced back to 1882, when rivalry about the superiority of Hereford, Short-horn, Angus, and Galloway cattle prompted stockmen to hold the Kansas City Fat Stock Show exhibit. In 1888, Kirkland Armour, owner of the meat-packing company and a breeder of Hereford cattle, organized the American Hereford Breeder's Association to encourage purebred-cattle. Herefords were exhibited under a tent south of the stockyards. The event was so successful that breeders of other cattle began participating in the annual exhibit, which evolved into the American Royal.

The latter's name came from an interview with a noted livestock judge in *The Daily Drovers Telegram* newspaper. The judge had attended the British Royal livestock shows in England and told the reporter that the cattle shows in the Kansas City stockyards compared favorably with their British counterparts. On New Year's Day, 1901, Walter P. Neff, editor of the newspaper, wrote an editorial titled "Call It The American Royal," and that became the name.

The Royal was held under tents until 1909, when the Stockyards company built a 55,000-square-foot steel frame structure at 19th and Wyandotte Streets. This building, called The American Royal Pavilion, was used for horse shows and stock judging; exhibits were still housed in tents.

As the Royal attracted more participants and audiences, it gradually outgrew the Pavilion. The shows were moved to Convention Hall at 13th and Central and then to Electric Park at 47th and The Paseo. But the Royal belonged in the stockyards. In 1921 the Kansas City Chamber of Commerce, three stock breeders associations, and the Stockyard Association raised $700,000 to construct a new American Royal Pavilion at

This old American Royal structure constructed in 1922 was torn down in 1992 to make way for the new American Royal compound.

Wyoming and 23rd streets. It was large enough that all of the Royal's activities could take place under one roof. November 18, 1922, saw the opening of the new building, and that year's Royal featured a performance of Handel's *Messiah.*

On February 13, 1925, there was an automobile show in the Pavilion. No one was in the building when a fire broke out, engulfing the building and destroying it. Kansas City's leaders vowed to build a new Pavilion on the old one's ruins. A heavier steel building with additional exhibit space and expanded seating was ready by that fall's American Royal.

Since 1928, the Future Farmers of America have planned their convention in Kansas City to correspond with the Royal, meeting the week before the Royal opens. Each year thousands of blue-jacketed young men and women from farm communities all over the United States descend on Kansas City to learn the latest about farming and ranching. It is one of the biggest conventions held in the city.

By the 1990s the old American Royal building had grown shabby and again become too small. It was torn down in January 1992 to make way for a new building that was ready for that fall's main event. The American Royal continues to be the world's largest combined livestock, horse show, and rodeo.

But the stockyards are no longer there. By the 1960s large feedlots were locating closer to large farms and cattle ranches, and meat-processing plants were established in many Midwest and Western states. Thus, there was no longer a need to centralize the cattle and pork industry. The Kansas City Stockyards were closed in 1991 and the pens dismantled. Today a 120-foot metal sculpture of cattle silhouettes sits across from the American Royal entrance, and life-size metal cutouts of cattle stand a few blocks away. They are eerie reminders of bygone days.

However, a few cattle traders still work out of the Livestock Exchange Building, and Mennonites still arrive at the City Market on Saturdays to sell vegetables and homemade breads, jams, and preserves.

Joseph McCoy, who had been promised a commission for each head of cattle driven over his trail, said that he was never compensated adequately for the millions of cattle that he shipped to the stockyards. He died almost penniless in a downtown Kansas City rooming house in 1915, forgotten as the founder of Kansas City's livestock trade.

STEAM, WHEELS, AND WINGS

The first travelers came here on foot. Indians paddled canoes. The Chouteaus journeyed aboard a flat-keel boat. The next wave started arriving on horseback and in wagons. Within a short time steamboats would unload thousands of passengers at the levee. After the Civil War, trains would bring new settlers to town—adventurers, merchants, and immigrants from all over the world. By the time Kansas City was 100 years old, airplanes were bringing the new arrivals.

The 1850s were called "The Golden Era of Steamboats" in Kansas City's history. The Missouri River was the freeway of its time. Traffic was so heavy on the river that vessels had to line up and wait to unload. For some of the steamboats, this town was the final destination; others would stop overnight and then proceed on up the river to towns in Northern Missouri, Nebraska, and Iowa. Although steam traffic would diminish considerably after 1870, boats would continue to dock at the levee at the bottom of Grand Avenue until the beginning of the 20th century.

The *Western Engineer* was the first steamboat to make it from St. Louis up the Missouri River as far as Fort Osage in 1819. Reportedly the Indians who saw it thought the boat was some kind of river monster. On the boat's bow was a sculptured figure of a scaly black snake with protruding red eyes, and steam hissed out of the snake's mouth. When the steamboat blew its whistle, the Indians had enough and ran into the woods.

The town's levee, formed by rocks jutting out into the river, was ideal for boat landings. By 1850, when the Missouri River wasn't frozen over, as many as 20 of these boats would arrive every week at the levee. It was a busy place. In 1857 the wharfmaster's record listed 725 boats arriving. Most of these vessels carried passengers as well as freight. Thirty passenger packet boats ran between St. Louis and the Town of Kansas throughout the year, stopping at towns along the way. Those who traveled on these smaller crafts carried their own food and bedding, and the trip took two or three weeks. Many of the passengers got off here to continue overland by wagon.

Passengers on the larger first-class boats traveled in luxury and the trip was faster, only two and a half to three days to make the trip from St. Louis. Tickets cost $25 and the boats could accommodate as many as 300 passengers in cabins on the upper decks. Cargo was carried below.

These steamboats were floating palaces. Their owners were proud of the rich furnishings, carpeted floors, elegant dining rooms, ornate bars, and expert cooks. The boats coming and going gave the riverfront community something to celebrate. Each vessel's whistle had a different sound or rhythm. When a boat would come around the bend downriver from the town, the crew would sound a loud whistle. Everyone knew which boat was on its way and townspeople would rush down to the levee to see who would get off and what cargo was to be unloaded.

Many of these boats carried a string orchestra made up of slave musicians. The captain would send word ahead that when his boat docked for the night, there would be dancing aboard and all were invited. This was a way some of young people courted. Parents would bring their daughters dressed in their newest hoopskirts. The town's young men would clean up and put on their best suits. Boy would meet girl and they would dance until after midnight.

The river could be treacherous, and some steamboats didn't finish the trip. Traveling the Missouri River was so hazardous that insurance coverage was difficult to get. It was estimated that the average life of a steamboat was 10 years, and many sank in the vicinity of Kansas City. Some said it wasn't always the fault of the river but rather reckless captains who liked to take chances. Steamboats sank for a variety of rea-

Even at the turn of the 20th century, steamboats were still docking at the levee at the bottom of Grand Avenue.

sons—they caught fire, their boilers exploded, they ran into rocks, or during the winter they became wedged in by ice jams. The most frequent cause of sinking was a submerged tree limb or trunk that pierced the steamer's hull.

This is what happened to the steamboat *Arabia*. This side-wheel steamboat left St. Louis in late August 1856 bound for Omaha, Nebraska, with a stopover scheduled at the Town of Kansas. There were 130 passengers aboard, mostly women with children going to meet their husbands who were building a town in Nebraska. The boat also carried a large cargo of foodstuffs, household goods, medical supplies, and lumber. It was like a floating store.

The *Arabia* stopped at the levee and then continued on the Missouri River. At the confluence of the Kaw it turned north toward Omaha. Traveling just a short distance farther, near the town of Parkville, the *Arabia* ran into a tree below the water surface. It began to sink immediately. Passengers jumped from the deck, and those who could swam to shore; others were picked out of the water by the crew in lifeboats. All were saved.

But the cargo went down with the boat. Because the river changed channels over the years, confusion arose about the exact location of the sunken *Arabia*. Tales of the boat's treasure, not only the cargo rumored to include 400 barrels of whiskey but also a supposed fortune in gold and silver, prompted several searches. But it wasn't until 132 years after it disappeared that the *Arabia* was found and its cargo salvaged.

Tall tales had circulated for years about the boat's resting place, but in 1988 the most unlikely story proved to be true. The *Arabia* was buried under farmland in Wyandotte County, Kansas, one-half mile from the present Missouri River. Over the years, floods and work done on the river to stop the flooding had rerouted the current and left the boat on dry land, covered with layers of silt, sand, and soil.

River Salvage, Inc., based in Independence, Missouri, used all the latest technology to unearth the *Arabia*. During a year-long process, the excavation pit took on the dimensions of a deep football field. Finally the deck was uncovered and the boat's treasures unveiled. However, no gold or silver or barrels of whiskey were found. What was there, preserved by the sand and silt, were everyday items available in general stores on the frontier in 1856: hardware, tools, bottled pickles, dishes, mirrors, flintlock rifles, handmade boots, hats, clothing, and trade goods from around the world. Over the next two years the salvagers painstakingly went about excavating, cleaning, and preserving the artifacts.

The Arabia Museum opened during the fall of 1991 in the Rivermarket area, close to the levee where the boat docked before its last run up the Missouri. The thousands of artifacts on display are only a fraction of what was found. More to be cleaned and repaired remains in storage, and the salvagers say it will probably take 25 years to do it all. The Arabia Museum is like a trip in a time machine. Articles displayed give the experience of everyday life on the frontier during Kansas City's golden years of the steamboat.

Besides wagons, those who chose to travel by land could take stagecoaches. By 1860 there were five lines operating out of a stagecoach depot at Second and Main. Passengers could board coaches to West Port, Independence, and other towns in Missouri and Kansas Territory. Travelers took stagecoaches to Cameron and St. Joseph to make connections with the Hannibal Railroad before the bridge was built that would bring that train into the Town of Kansas.

The Butterfield Stage departed from here on its way to Santa Fe, New Mexico. Because it carried the mail, the line was subsidized by the government; however, passengers still had to pay $175 in gold for a one-way ticket. The stagecoaches often carried shipments of Mexican gold and silver to and from Santa Fe, and the route went through Indian Territory. Eight armed guards usually rode on top of these coaches. Each man had at his side a Colt revolving rifle, a shotgun, two Colt revolvers, and a hunting knife. The guards could get off over 100 shots without reloading in case of attack.

The coaches were built sturdy to withstand the rocky terrain and they were airtight to keep the water out when rolling through streams and creeks. With the armed guards riding shotgun, each coach could only accommodate 6 to 8 passengers comfortably, but the company claimed 12 would fit. The stagecoach left Second and Main every Saturday morning at 7 a.m.

It took 22 days and nights of constant riding to get to Santa Fe. Horses were exchanged every 25 miles. Passengers paid a dollar for meals and were given an hour to eat in coach stations along the way. The typical menu was flapjacks and coffee for breakfast and buffalo steak with dried apples for lunch and dinner. Travelers were each allowed 40 pounds of baggage. At $175 for a one-way ticket, with the threat of Indian raids and outlaw hold-ups, three weeks in cramped quarters without being able to take a bath, a bumpy ride, and a steady diet of buffalo meat, stagecoach travelers must have really wanted to go to Santa Fe.

The coming of the railroads to the Town of Kansas ended stagecoach travel, drastically reduced the steamboat business, and implemented the death of the Santa Fe Trail trade after the Civil War.

Construction on the Pacific Railroad (later the Missouri Pacific) began in St. Louis in 1852. The push westward was slow. It took more than 10 years to lay the track 188 miles to Sedalia, Missouri, then the outbreak of the Civil War stopped construction. Bushwackers from Kansas robbed railroad contractors, took horses, mules, and wagons, and threatened tracklayers. As Confederate General Sterling Price's troops marched through Missouri in 1864, they destroyed 13 bridges, 4 locomotives, and 39 freight cars, plus they blew up machine shops and water towers, and ripped up miles of steel track.

After the war, it was time to start over. While one construction crew laid track coming west, another was putting down rails moving east from the Town of Kansas. The two tracks met just east of Independence, Missouri. The last spike was hammered into the connecting rail on September 19, 1865. The next day a train left the Town of Kansas for St. Louis.

That train had arrived a year before by boat. An engine, four flat cars, and 100 tons of rail came to the town aboard the steamboat *McGill.* The investors who brought the train here included Alexander Majors, Pierre Chouteau, John McCoy, and others who had made money in the Santa Fe trade. They realized that, if the town was to have a future in trade, this one track and small train was the first step. The track was connected to the one laid east of town, then the train was hoisted onto the track, ready to roll. When that final spike was driven in, the train moved out for its first trip East. The investors and town officials were all aboard, and they got off at the Little Blue River to have a celebration picnic.

Across the state line, the Kansas Pacific began track construction in 1863 and a year later trains were running to Lawrence and Wyandotte, (now Kansas City, Kansas). The State Line Depot was constructed on the west bank of the Kaw River, which enabled limited shipments of cattle to come into the early stockyards located near the depot. After the Missouri Pacific line was connected to the Town of Kansas, the company paid Kansas Pacific $25,000 for right-of-way land so track could be laid running west from the levee around the bend into the West Bottoms.

Meanwhile the Hannibal, St. Joseph Railroad had completed their track across northern Missouri, making connections with St. Louis and

Chicago. Prior to 1867, local travelers had to either go to Weston, Missouri, by steamboat or ferry across the Missouri to Harlem, directly across from the levee, and then take a stagecoach to St. Joseph or Cameron to board the train Hannibal train. In 1867 the Hannibal company extended their line directly to Harlem, but the train was still a ferry ride away from the Town of Kansas, which limited large amounts of freight shipments

Leavenworth and the Town of Kansas were in fierce competition to get the first railway bridge to span the Missouri River. Leavenworth had taken over the origination point of the Santa Fe trade during the Civil War and now saw itself as surpassing Kansas City as the trade center of the Midwest. With the military fort nearby, this Kansas community had a lot of clout in Washington, where a bill was to be introduced in Congress concerning post offices and post roads and bridges to be constructed across the Mississippi River. Leavenworth hoped to include their bridge in the bill.

Those who had invested in the first train realized that the Town of Kansas had to get the bridge to survive. The city council refused to call an election to vote on bridge bonds, so a citizen meeting was called. Supporters of the bridge spoke to the large gathering, and $28,000 was raised that night. At a meeting four days later, another $41,000 was raised to buy the land. Feeling this was enough to convince the board of the Hannibal, St. Joseph Railroad to invest their money building the bridge, a delegation from the town went to Boston to lobby Hannibal's board of directors. The contingent took with them a drawing of what they hoped the bridge would look like. The railroad owners were impressed and said if the bill passed Congress, they would build the bridge and their railroad would connect the Town of Kansas with Chicago.

Meanwhile, Missouri congressman and former mayor Robert T. Van Horn drafted an amendment to the bill to include a bridge across the Missouri that favored the Town of Kansas location. Meeting with the chairman of the committee that oversaw the post offices, Van Horn persuaded him that the Town of Kansas was better situated to be a mail center than was Leavenworth. And since the mail would be carried by trains, it followed that the bridge would make mail delivery quicker. The bridge was granted to the Missouri community. It was to be located at about where Broadway is today.

Building the mile-long bridge across a river known for fast currents and flooding was a challenge made even more so because the little town had only one foundry and one small machine shop. But Octave

Chanute, who was hired to design, plan, and build the bridge, not only knew railroads (he had been chief engineer for the Chicago and Alton line) but could design the required tools and set up the shops to make them. Chanute found the limestone rocks needed for the piers in local quarries and had timbers cut from forests across the river in order to build the superstructure for the bridge. He improvised new techniques and inspired the builders. Construction started in 1867, and the bridge took two years to complete.

Old timers told Chanute stories about the 1844 flood's 48-foot crest level, so he designed the bridge 11 feet higher. In the first attempt to put the support piers in place on the shifting sand of the riverbottom, the swift current tilted them over. Chanute then designed more sturdy piers, basing them on a design that had been used in a bridge spanning the Rhine River in Germany. Workers in diving suits anchored long wooden shafts into the sand that were then driven deep by a pile-driver powered by a horse walking in circles. This time the piers held. Chanute also built a watertight chamber for workers so they could be lowered into the river. Divers dressed in rubber suits and, wearing helmets with air hoses connected to the surface, could only work a limited amount of time on the river's bottom to secure the piers in the sand.

Divers ready to go underwater to secure the Hannibal Bridge's piers.

To relax, Octave Chanute would fly kites from the bluffs overlooking the north bank of the river. In the 1890s, when he turned 60 years old, he started building multi-wing gliders. Using his experience as a structural engineer, Chanute built some of the strongest and lightest gliders of his day. He also acted as an early consultant to aviation pioneers Wilbur and Orville Wright.

The bridge's official opening day was Saturday, July 3, 1869. Before daybreak, people came on foot, on horseback, in carriages, and wagons. All morning, long passenger trains arrived and unloaded at the Second and Grand and the State Line depots, and at the Harlem station across the Missouri River. Governors from five states, 21 mayors from cities throughout the Midwest, and officials from all the country's great railroads came to the celebration. It was reported that on this day the town swelled to 40,000 people. All wanted to celebrate the great occasion. A parade of brass bands and military drill teams marched through the streets of the town.

Carriages rolled along the parade route full of the town's leaders, their important guests, and the day's special hero: Octave Chanute. Crowds of people stood on top of every hill and hundreds deep in every street to see the opening ceremonies. As they cheered, the procession halted at the southern end of the bridge. The magnificent engine, "The Hannibal," slowly pulling 10 of the most elegantly appointed train cars ever made, came from the north side of the bridge. The town's train pulled out from the southern end. As the two came to the center of the bridge they stopped and blew their whistles. The bridge was officially open. The crowd roared and surged forward to inspect the impressive span. Looking out of every window, standing on top of every hill, pouring into every street, hundreds deep to see the opening ceremonies. They knew that this great bridge had been accomplished against enormous odds. They were proud of the bridge, proud of their town and proud of themselves. They called it "The Immortal Bridge", "The Kansas City Bridge", or with reverence, just, "The Bridge". (It wasn't called the Hannibal Bridge until later.)

Festivities continued all day. The town's balloonist released his aircraft, labeled "Kansas City Progress," and glided to Independence. That afternoon, at 12th and Troost, there was a public picnic. Everyone was invited. The town paid for barbecue and other food that was spread out on many long tables, reportedly there was enough so that all who came to see the bridge's opening got fed. That night a banquet was held at a hotel at Fifth and Broadway for the dignitaries and investors. Chanute was the honored guest. A 10-foot-long cake in the shape of the bridge was served. After endless toasts and speeches, everyone called the bridge the greatest achievement so far in the city's history.

Completion of the bridge not only brought the Hannibal Railway into town, but shortly seven other major railroads extended their tracks to connect with the span. By 1881, 15 trains used the bridge. Although damaged in an 1886 tornado and 1903 flood, it was repaired and used until 1917 when a new bridge was built next to it. This two-level structure not only allowed trains to cross the Missouri River, but automobiles also traveled on the upper level. Soon after the newer bridge opened, the old was torn down.

With the opening of the Hannibal Bridge bringing more trains into town, it was soon apparent that the small depots couldn't handle the increased volume of traffic. Leaders started talking about a new, larger depot, but by 1875 the city was on the verge of bankruptcy because over $400,000 in taxes were delinquent. A new City Charter was written that provided, among other things, penalties against delinquent taxpayers. Almost immediately, taxes were paid and the city's credit was restored.

In 1877 construction began on a much larger depot on land owned by Kersey Coates in the West Bottoms. It was to be called Union Depot. That location was near the stockyards and the meat packers who needed direct rail connections to receive cattle from the West and to ship out meat to the North and East.

The builder, James McConigle, had erected smaller depots and was constructing a mental hospital in Topeka at the same time he was to build Union Depot. When civic leaders saw the magnitude of the proposed depot's rambling design, they called it "Kansas City's Insane Asylum." Many thought it was too big: there wouldn't be enough trains, passengers, or freight to make use of it. Luckily, others had faith in the growth of the city's commerce and the design got the go-ahead. Two years after the depot was completed, an annex had to be constructed in order to accommodate the high volume of rail traffic.

When the Union Depot opened April 8, 1878, it still prompted criticism. The design was supposed to resemble a French palace with many towers, turrets, arches, cupolas, and architectural ornaments. Some called the conglomeration of Gothic and Victorian styles a "sprawling monstrosity." Its appearance wasn't enhanced by the coal-burning trains; they belched black smoke that soon covered the building inside and out.

The depot was located right on Union Avenue. To cross the street,

The Union Depot in the West Bottoms at the turn-of the-century.

pedestrians had to step over many crisscrossed tracks and dodge oncoming trains. Passengers with time to kill and those who walked to catch the cable car to downtown Kansas City had to sidestep more than trains. The street was known for every kind of sin that could entice travelers and the cowboys who came to the stockyards. Two blocks in any direction from the depot were so many saloons that it looked like a continuous bar. There were also gambling halls, sleazy hotels, pawn shops, penny arcades, billiard halls and tattoo parlors, and seedy brothels, plus street hustlers who prowled the street, looking for suckers to fleece.

If this wasn't enough to make the newcomer apprehensive, the prospect of riding on the elevated Ninth Street Incline out of the Bottoms was. The Incline was built in 1885 by streetcar owner Robert Gillham, who admired San Francisco's cable car system. The cars were propelled by an underground moving cable under the track connected to a central power station. The ride was a breath taking plunge from Quality Hill to the Bottoms on a track that was almost at a 90-degree angle. Although the structure supporting the incline looked like it could collapse at any time, in its 10 years of operation there were few accidents. But that couldn't be said of the trip coming from the other direction.

The Ninth Street car began east of downtown, making many sharp turns and descending quickly down hills as it made its way west to Grand

Riding the Ninth Street Incline in and out of West Bottoms was not for the faint of heart.

Avenue. From there the ride proceeded down a steeper hill to The Junction, the intersection of Ninth and Main. Because the brakes on these cars weren't always reliable, they came into the intersection so fast that they often jumped off their cables, hurling passengers out of their seats, injuring pedestrians, and frightening the horses pulling nearby carriages.

To protect themselves from lawsuits, owners of the cable line hired the first traffic cop in the city. His job was to alert all in the intersection of Ninth and Main that the cable car was descending the hill and that they should get out of the way. When he saw a car coming, the patrolman would frantically yell "Wide-a-Wake! Wide-a-Wake!" When people didn't move fast enough, he grabbed them and move them out of the way. The Ninth Street Incline was razed in 1905.

The 1903 flood filled the Union Depot with water for a week. Passengers and freight trains couldn't get in or out. Because the increased railroad traffic had almost outgrown the old depot, city leaders had been talking for some time about building a new terminal on the same site. But the flood decided the matter. The next depot had to be located on safer ground and be more accessible to passenger traffic.

The planners decided to build Union Station on land west of Grand Avenue at 23rd Street. The project took many meetings and planning sessions. Twelve railroads that would use the station organized into the Kansas City Terminal Railroad Company. The company would pay a total of over $50 million to build the depot. They were given a 200-year franchise and paid the city a half million for the Grand Avenue land.

As designed, the building would cost $5.8 million. Over 40 streets had to be vacated to widen the old Belt Line Railway channel surrounding the city so that 32 tracks could be laid to bring trains in and out of the station. Viaducts would be built over these tracks. OK Creek, the stream Santa Fe wagons had to ford, would be diverted into large pipes under the tracks. Construction began in 1912.

Union Station, with its vast underground terminal and the land occupied by the tracks coming into it, was the third largest railroad station in the world (second only to New York's Grand Central and Pennsylvania stations). The waiting rooms alone could comfortably accommodate thousands of people.

The new depot took two years to build. The Commercial Club (later the Chamber of Commerce) sponsored a three-day celebration for its opening. On Friday afternoon, October 30, 1914, a battery of cannons located across the street fired a 21-gun salute to signal that Union Station was officially open. Over 100,000 people, nearly one-half of the city's population, waited outside. As the doors opened the crowd surged into

Union Station under construction.

the station. They went everywhere: through the lobby and waiting room and down the stairs to inspect the underground tracks. Few heard the speakers at the ribbon cutting. Many waited in line at the ticket counter (which wouldn't open until 11 p.m.) to buy tickets for the first trains to leave the station. That evening there was a masked ball in the station's waiting room, and in attendance were governors from surrounding states. The parades, crowds, and celebrations continued through the weekend.

Union Depot was abandoned the night after the new station opened. Many thought it appropriate that the last train out of the old dirty building would leave on Halloween night. That depot was demolished in 1915 and with that came the demise of Union Avenue. Today there is no trace that the station ever existed in the West Bottoms.

Union Station played an important part in the wars Americans fought during the first half of the 20th century. Soldiers going off to the First and Second World Wars and then the Korean War all left and returned home through the station.

People gathered in the new station, not just to board trains or welcome travelers home but for other reasons, too. The big clock in the

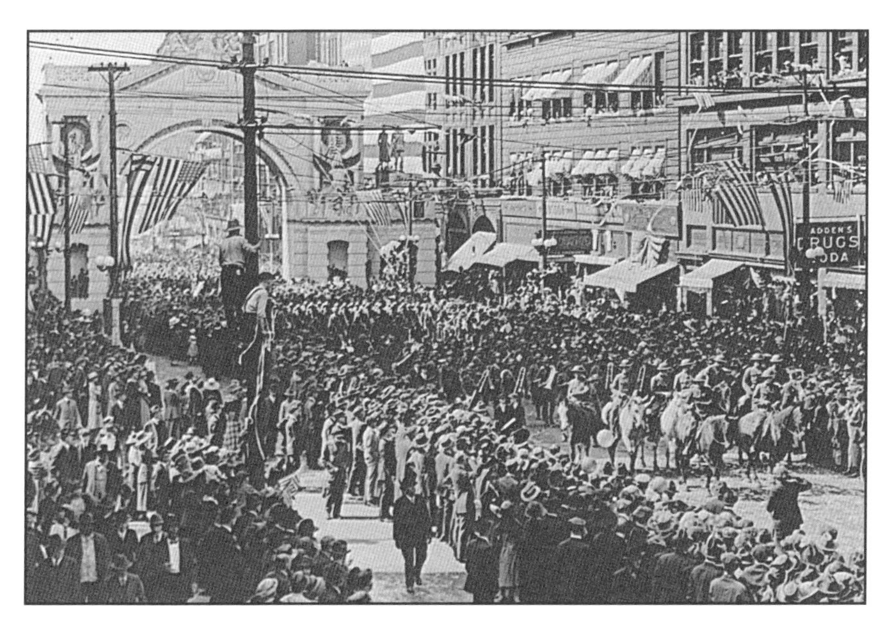

Soldiers returning home from the First World War marched from Union Station, down Grand Avenue through a large "Victory Arch" built in the middle of Grand Avenue between 10th to 11th.

lobby was a popular rendezvous place for lovers and friends. People came to buy newspapers from around the world at the lobby's newsstand. Many came to the station for a meal—the Fred Harvey Coffee Shop, The Westport Room, and the cafeteria at the north end of the lobby were all popular eating places. And when newspapers announced that celebrities would be coming to town, many would flock to the station to see the arriving movie stars, presidents of the United States, foreign heads of state, and sports figures.

By the late 1940s, over 200 passenger trains a day rolled into the station. But by the 1950s almost everyone could afford a car, and people were driving to vacation spots and on business trips. Air travel was becoming less expensive and took far less time than the train. Freight was being shipped by air, too, and large trucking firms could haul small freight between cities at a cheap rate. Train use declined. By the end of the 1950s less than 20 trains a day were leaving the station.

Soon, so few trains were using Union Station that the Terminal Railroad Company decided it wasn't feasible to heat it. For several years Amtrak ran a small operation in the lobby, but the rest of the station was sealed off by a giant plastic bubble made to conserve the heat. Amtrak then moved down below onto the platform near the train tracks and the station was closed in 1983. But trains kept coming through the city and today the rail traffic through Kansas City is second only to Chicago.

The grand old station had suffered many indignities but perhaps what happened next was the worse. In 1974 the city entered into an agreement with a developer who wanted to erect several office buildings on land east of the station. The agreement was that the city would provide tax breaks for the new structures on the condition that the builders would rehabilitate the station. The buildings went up and the tax abatement given, but nothing was done to the station. Beginning in 1988 the city instigated a long, drawn-out lawsuit against the developer, asking for $91 million for breach of contract. The case took almost five years. The city finally got 20 acres of land surrounding the station and $1.5 million, about a third of what it had cost Kansas City in legal fees fighting the case. The lawsuit also directed that the station be turned over to a nonprofit corporation.

Many uses have been suggested for the station: a United Nations museum, a transportation museum, a large botanical garden, and even a gambling casino. The Kansas City Museum's plan to put a science museum in the station has received enthusiastic support. Some money from various sources has been pledged to restore the station, however, at this writing much more is needed.

The automobile was introduced to Kansas City right after the turn of the century. In 1901 there were two cars in town and they managed to collide with one another near 11th and Oak. Newspaper accounts said that the drivers, coming in opposite directions at 15 miles per hour, saw each other but refused to pull over to allow the other car to pass.

Cars were being made in Kansas City as early as 1903, the same year that Henry Ford started producing his first model. That year John Caps opened a factory on Southwest Boulevard to build a two-cylinder auto that sold for $800. The vehicle sold so well that he built a larger factory, costing $100,000, near the Blue River. In 1905 Caps started experimenting with four-and six-cylinder cars, using designs and technology from European models. His larger cylinder cars proved costly to produce and this put them out of the range of local buyers. Caps went broke and became a mechanic. Several other early manufacturers also built cars here, including Woods Electric Company, which produced electric cars that ran for 100 miles without having to recharge the batteries.

Auto making on a grand scale came to Kansas City in 1909, when the Ford Motor Company opened a plant in the Blue Valley industrial district near the Kansas City Nut and Bolt Steel Mill (later to become Sheffield Steel, and now ARMCO), so that the latter could supply the raw material needed to build the cars.

Steadily, more people began buying cars. In 1920 there were 244,000 auto licenses issued in Missouri, and the Ford plant was enlarged several times to meet the demand. By 1928 the 1,250 auto workers at the Ford plant produced over 300 Model A's a day.

The Ford plant's location, close to Sheffield Steel and near railroad shipping connections to all parts of the country, soon attracted another major car manufacturer. In 1918 General Motors spent $2.5 million to build a Fisher Body factory and a Chevrolet plant in nearby Leeds.

Even during the Depression, automakers made big profits, but their auto workers only made 45 cents an hour. After Congress passed the Wagner Act in 1933, allowing the right of workers to organize and bargain collectively, automakers still fought unionizing the industry. Worker dissatisfaction continued to grow.

The first sit-down strike against an automaker in this country occurred in the Kansas City Fisher Body plant. On December 16, 1936, a thousand employees stopped working and sat down in protest against

General Motors' opposition to unionizing. They wouldn't leave the plant. They organized their own fire and police force, musical groups, and barber shops, and even held church services inside. General Motors turned off the heat in the building and tried to bribe the men by offering them a Christmas bonus if they came out. That didn't work. Management then threatened the strikers with police action.

With the stoppage at Fisher Body, Chevrolet workers ran out of auto bodies and that plant shut down. On December 23, these workers joined the protest and put up a picket line outside their building.

The Kansas City strike sparked sit-down action across the country that closed down seven General Motors plants. Striking auto workers even closed down the company's birthplace plant at Flint, Michigan. Auto making was Flint's principal industry, and the owners had the support of city officials as well as the newspapers. Newswriters inflamed the public and soon there were outbreaks of violence on both sides. A Kansas City contingent joined thousands of auto workers from all over the country who traveled to Flint to picket the plants. The police fired buckshot and lobbed tear gas into the mob. The National Guard arrived with fixed bayonets and loaded guns to face the picketers. Michigan's governor, Frank Murphy, fearing escalation of the violence and bloodshed, compelled the automakers to sit down and talk with union officials.

After over two months of striking, an agreement was reached February 17, 1937. The United Auto Workers Union was recognized, and over 200,000 workers rushed to join. Kansas City workers returned to their plants in Leeds. Later they received a 30-cent per hour raise negotiated by their union.

General Motors no longer has a factory in the Kansas City area, but Ford Motor Company produces cars at the Claycomo plant north of the Missouri River, and there is a Buick/Pontiac plant located in the Kansas City, Kansas, Fairfax industrial district. Today the metropolitan area ranks sixth in the nation in auto assembly.

The city's aviation history started with the balloon ascent to celebrate the opening of the Hannibal Bridge in 1869. Later, balloonists came to town and offered rides. Such an interest grew in the sport that a balloon union, The Kansas City Aeronauts Local #1, was formed in 1910. An international balloon race was held here in 1911, drawing nine balloonists from around the world to compete for a first prize of $1,500 for landing the greatest distance from Kansas City. Fifty thousand spectators cheered as the balloons took off from the riverfront near Holmes Street. Compliments of a local liquor store, each balloonist carried an assortment of wine and whiskey. The German balloon won by landing in Wisconsin three days later.

The first airplane took flight here in 1909 from Overland Park, Kansas, just to the south of Kansas City. The owner of the Strang Interurban Railroad wanted to attract Kansas Citians to take his railroad line to Overland Park. He contracted with a pilot to bring his biplane from St. Louis for the event. A crowd took Mr. Strang's train to see the plane take off. In the first attempt, the plane's wheels had just left the dirt when its tail struck a post, but the pilot was able to land safely. The next day the plane took off again and soared to a height of 500 feet.

In the next several years various barnstormers (pilots who went from town to town, landing in farm pastures) flew into Kansas City to demonstrate their flying ability and give plane rides for a price. Barnstorming would continue here even into the 1930s.

Airplane technology advanced with the United States' entry into World War I. Planes were made to fly better and longer in order to win in "dogfights," serve as observers for artillery targets, and be successful on bombing raids. The First World War taught young men to fly, and many who already knew how became trainers.

Lieutenant John F. Richards II, who was born in Kansas City, learned to fly at the Aviation Training School at Austin, Texas. He sailed for France on August 15, 1917, and was assigned to the pioneer corps of the Air Force, Aero Squadron No. 1. He successfully participated in several aerial battles, but on September 26, 1918, he was killed when his plane was shot down over the Argonne Forest. On Armistice Day, 1922, Kansas City dedicated its first real airfield, naming it after Lieutenant Richards. The field was built with $150,000 of federal money and $100,000 raised by the Kansas City Air Terminal Association. Richards Field, located in south Kansas City near 87th and Blue Ridge Road, also became the Army Air Corps Reserve field. In 1943 the airport was sold to Bill Ong, who had been a winner in air races in the 1930s. During World War II Ong trained 7,200 Army pilots at the field. After the war, with the increased need for new homes for returning veterans, the airfield land was developed as a housing project.

Air races were big in the 1920s. On November 21, 1921, an American Legion aerial race was held at Legion Field (55th and Belinder), today a part of Mission Hills, Kansas. Forty-five thousand people gathered to see 13 planes fly 10 laps at fast speed around pylons. Pilots participated in these races all across the country, and many built their own planes. Kansas Citian Ed Porterfield built the American Eagle A-1 in a rented garage on Prospect Avenue. He sold several of these planes, and by 1927 American Eagle Aircraft had orders for over 200 Eagles. Porterfield expanded his operation several times. After one of the owners of General Motors bought stock, Porterfield built a large factory in Kansas City, Kansas, that employed 115 workers. His planes sold so well that later he sold out to the General Motors stockholder.

In 1925, federal legislation passed that would pay civilian airplane companies to carry the mail. Kansas City's Richards Field became one of the first airports to have regularly scheduled airmail flights. However, because there were several crashes at the field and pilots expressed safety concerns, soon the government would not allow mail flights in or out of Richards.

The Air Corps Reserve Officers Association of Greater Kansas City, made up of 100 former officers who fought in World War I, met with the chamber of commerce to try to get the city to invest in a first-class airport. The chamber's president, Lou Holland, was instrumental in persuading the city administration that another location for the airport was needed. The reserve officers surveyed the area for a likely landing field site. The site that met all of their criteria was 697 acres of land on the north side of the river, by the confluence of the Missouri and Kaw Rivers, close to the old city of Harlem where people used to go by ferry to catch stagecoaches and make train connections.

Some wanted to call the airport Peninsula Field, because part of it jutted out into the Missouri River. The Reserve Officers wanted it to bear the name of Lieutenant Richards. As a compromise, the main road into the airport was called Richards Road. A lease was negotiated with the North Kansas City Development Company with an option to buy. But the airport was nothing but open field when Charles Lindbergh came for the dedication on August 17, 1927.

Just three months before, Lindbergh had flown his plane, the *Spirit of St. Louis*, on the first nonstop solo flight from New York to Paris. He was a national hero. Everywhere he went thousands of people were waiting to get a glimpse of "Lindy." Kansas Citians were no different—6,000 were waiting for him along the cleared path that was the airport's runway. When Lindbergh flew in, he thought the spectators were too close for a safe landing. He zoomed down and pulled up, circling, looking for some place to land. The crowd thought he was performing for them and cheered. He came down on a soggy field to the north of the runway. The jubilant crowd rushed through the mud toward him. Lindbergh grabbed a stick from the ground to protect himself and his plane. Luckily, U.S. Army soldiers reached him before the fans did and formed a wedge to get him through the crowd and into an open car. Lindbergh was wearing the same leather jacket he wore on his flight to Paris.

Lindbergh's car joined a parade through downtown to the Muehlebach Baseball Field at 22nd and Brooklyn, where he was to give a speech. The parade route was lined with people waving and yelling. It was estimated that up to 100,000 saw the famous pilot that day. That evening he visited with aviator friends from Fort Leavenworth and flew out of town the next morning.

The voters had to approve a bond issue of a million dollars in order to buy the land, build a small terminal and four hangers, and surface the two runways with cinders. The election was scheduled in May 1928. To attract votes, air shows were given for the public. They liked the shows but the bonds failed. In August the bonds were submitted again, and this time they were approved. Work thus began on the Municipal Airport.

A year later the first passenger plane left the new airport, now called the Kansas City Airport. A passenger terminal was constructed, and the city proclaimed to the world that it was "the air center of the United States". That year Transcontinental Air Transport (later Transcontinental & Western Air—TWA) made this airport their headquarters. The reclusive Howard Hughes, a major stockholder in the airline, often flew into the airport to check up on the company. He always piloted his own aircraft, arriving late at night and sleeping in his plane.

By the late 1930s, Mid-Continent Airlines and Braniff Airways also had bases here. In 1938 three of the cinder runways were paved with concrete and a larger main terminal came under construction. At the opening of the new building much was made of the fact that the airport was just five minutes away from downtown via the Hannibal Bridge built in 1917. (The lower level of that bridge still remains east of the Broadway Bridge.) However, it became easier to get to the airport once the Broadway Bridge was finished in 1957. It cost $12 million to build, with the plan that toll fees would pay off the debt (which was retired in 1991 and the toll booths were removed).

Private planes, flying schools, and even plane manufacturers were located at the airport. Major renovations in the late 1950s expanded the terminal and lengthened the runways to accommodate jet landings. In 1957, even though the city was talking about building Mid-Continent Airport, $4 million was spent on a new terminal building, a restaurant, and a parking lot. Over 200 planes, half of them jet passenger planes, used the airport every day.

In 1957 Richards Gebaur Air Force Base opened on the former Grandview airport site, west of Highway 71. The base was named after Lieutenant John F. Richards as well as another Kansas City resident, Lieutenant Colonel Arthur Gebaur, who was killed flying his plane on a mission in the Korean War. The base would become the second largest employer in the metropolitan area and would be responsible for the growth of Grandview, Missouri. The Air Force put on annual air shows at the air base, attracting huge crowds. The show after the Gulf War drew almost 800,000 to the field to see the planes perform. With the end of the Cold War and downsizing the military, the Air Force closed the base in 1994.

Kansas City started planning for Mid-Continent Airport in the late 1950s, the beginning of a long process. The site selected was a 4,700-acre area in Platte County, near I-29 north of Tiffany Springs.

Construction estimates started at $23 million. In 1966 Kansas City residents voted "yes" on a $150 million bond issue to construct the airport. The final price tag, however, was $250 million. Planners decided that the field would be called Kansas City International Airport.

The KCI design was considered an innovation because of its three circular terminals set some distance apart. Individual airlines were based in only one terminal, and signage on the main airport road alerted passengers to which airline was based in which terminal. Unlike most, these were designed so that people had just a short walk to check in at the ticket counter and the departing and incoming gates. The design idea was called a "Drive to Your Gate" system.

The starting date on the project was delayed many times. Property owners held out for more money. The city, needing additional space for the airport, proposed to annex the necessary land, but this was held up by lawsuits. Even after the construction started in 1968, there were delays because of weather, a 16-month labor strike, the collapse of a newly built control tower, and the enormous size of the project. It also took a while to sign up the airlines to lease the new terminal. Kansas City's international airport officially opened on November 21, 1972, and today 19 passenger airlines use it for over 250 flights a day.

The last commercial jet passenger flight left Municipal Airport the day that Kansas City International Airport opened. The year before, an advertisement appeared in aviation journals across the country offering the airport for lease. Respondents wanted to lease space but not the whole airport. Municipal became the airport that served business and pleasure aircraft. In 1977 it was renamed Kansas City Downtown Airport. After the 1993 flood, $8 million was spent to renovate the Downtown Airport. In 1994 a recorded 700 planes a day landed or took off from the airport.

An air museum operates in a terminal at the Downtown Airport. Save-A-Connie, a 400-member, nonprofit group, is dedicated to restoring vintage propeller passenger planes. All of the members have backgrounds in aviation, and many have helped to restore a Lockheed Super Constellation and a Martin 404, both of which flew passengers in the 1950s and 1960s out of the airport. These planes are taken to air shows across the country and have been used in major motion pictures.

This city was settled because its location provided easy access to the water highways of this country. As transportation technology has expanded, Kansas City has continued to be a transportation hub. The town of Lebanon, in the center of Kansas near the Nebraska state line, has been designated as the geographical center of continental United States. However, Kansas City, with its two airports making air travel connections to cities all over the world, can be said to be the nation's transportation center.

VILLAINS, HEROES, CELEBRITIES, AND OTHER FOLK

People and events define a city's history. And individuals' histories are often spoken about in terms of happening "before" or "after" an event in the city. Kansas City's past has numerous people and events that history remembers as interesting, curious, and intriguing.

The first black man in the area was a fellow named York, and he was among the 45 members of the Lewis and Clark expedition to explore the land west of the Mississippi River. York was William Clark's slave. The latter wrote in his journal that the group crossed through this area in June 1804 and camped for three days at the confluence of two rivers.

In 1830 Mormons came from the East to start a community in Independence, Missouri, believing that it would become the center of the Mormon faith. In 1831 Bishop Edward Partridge purchased land near today's Linwood Boulevard and along the north side of Brush Creek, west to the State Line. However, the Mormon's Evening and Morning Star newspaper published articles against a Missouri law that prohibited freed slaves from settling in the state. Jackson County settlers, mostly from the South, took these publications as encouragement for free blacks to come to the area. Anti-Mormon mobs took to the streets of Independence, destroying the Star's printing press and building. Mormon-owned businesses were looted and burned. The protestors captured Bishop Partridge and other Mormon leaders and tarred and feathered them.

Some of the Mormons left for Ohio, while others went to Clay County where they had friends. When mobs came to push those who remained in Jackson Country off their lands, they fought back. However, by 1834 the Mormons had been run out of Jackson County. The land on Brush Creek was sold to Alexander Doniphan, and then in 1858 the trader William Bent acquired it. The Battle of Westport was fought on and around this land. After Bent's death in 1868, the property was acquired by Seth Ward, whose family later donated some of the land for Ward Parkway.

When the call went out for volunteers to fight in the Mexican War of 1846, Missourians were the first to volunteer. Some came from Jackson County and bought their provisions for the journey from merchants in the Town of Kansas and West Port. In 1847 Alexander Doniphan and Stephen Kearney led a Missouri regiment of 1,164 men across the plains to take Santa Fe, New Mexico, with little resistance. Kearney then took his men west toward California. Doniphan's forces marched south across the arid desert and overcame an army that was four times their force in order to occupy El Paso, Chihuahua, and Sacramento.

One member of this army was a woman from Platte County. Disguised as a man, she fought in the battles alongside soldiers who thought she was "Bill Newcom." After the battles, on the way back to Missouri after long months of campaigning, someone disclosed to the commander, Major William Gilphin, that this was a woman in soldier's clothing. (Gilphin, who was from Independence, later became President Abraham Lincoln's bodyguard.)

In 1848 Elizabeth Newcom was "informally" discharged and returned home. Congress had passed an act that rewarded all who fought in the Mexican War with 160 acres of land. But it was deemed that Elizabeth, now Mrs. John Smith, wasn't eligible. She petitioned the Congressional Committee on Military Affairs. They investigated and issued a report that said "there is no doubt that the service was rendered and she is entitled to her pay, as the law makes no distinction with regard to sex; as her services were as useful to the government as if she had been a man." A private act was introduced on her behalf in Congress and she got her land in Atchison County, where she and her husband raised their children on their farm.

John McCoy wrote in his journal that Periault's wife killed John Gray in the French Settlement. This probably happened sometime in the 1840s. Gray, half Scot and half Iroquois, was a hunter and guide. McCoy noted that the woman was a member of the Snake Indian tribe and the only Indian he had seen with red hair. In his journal entry McCoy forgot to list the date, her name, or her motive for the killing.

In the March 1853 election, a city charter of incorporation was to be voted on as well as offices of mayor, city council, tax collector, city treasurer, and some others. The 30 men who voted were running for these offices. They voted for themselves and each other. William S. Gregory was elected mayor, but it was discovered that he hadn't lived in the city long enough to qualify. Another election was held and Dr. Johnston Lykins became mayor. The annual payroll for the city officers was a total of $1,000.

Senator Thomas Hart Benton (the great uncle and namesake of the 20th-century artist) said in a speech before the town's city council in 1854, "Here where the Missouri, after running its southward course for nearly 2,000 miles, turns eastward to the Mississippi, a large commercial and manufacturing community will congregate and in less than a generation we will see a great city on these hills." The hills were leveled in a generation. The great city took a little longer and is still evolving.

In 1855 Milton McGee, one of the town's leading citizens, was arrested for driving his horsedrawn buggy too fast on Main Street near the levee. He paid his fine, then the next day drove his buggy pulled by a yoke of oxen on the same street. As the oxen slowly crept along toward the river and back, the buggy created a traffic jam, much to McGee's amusement.

After Main Street was overrun with hogs in August 1858, a "Hog Law" was passed, authorizing the city's marshal to catch any of the porkers found roaming the streets and put them in the "Hog Pound." Forty swine were apprehended, and their owners had to pay a fine to get them out.

A Chess Club that met above a store on Third Street in 1860 had nearly 30 members. Not a traditional image of the Wild West!

In July 1863, soldiers of Brigadier General Thomas E. Ewing's 11th Kansas Volunteers stationed in the Town of Kansas arrested nine young women accused of carrying food, supplies, and information to Quantrill's Bushwhackers, who were terrorizing Missouri towns that were sympathetic to the Union. Ewing commandeered a building at 14th and Grand Avenue to serve as a prison for the women while they waited to be tried. Two weeks later the building collapsed and four of the prisoners were killed.

Why the building collapsed is still a mystery, but Quantrill believed it was caused intentionally by the Union troops. He saw that a rumor was circulated that the girls had been murdered. Quantrill took his revenge on Lawrence, Kansas, a town known for its support of the Union. On August 21, 1863, he led his troops to burn most of the town and killed about 150 people. Frank James rode with Quantrill that day. Jesse James joined Quantrill's band a short time later.

General Ewing retaliated by issuing Order No. 11, to stop the farmers in western Missouri from sheltering the Quantrill band and giving them supplies. The order mandated the evacuation of all Missouri farms in a three-county area (including Jackson County) within 15 days. Ewing was determined to burn the heart out of the Confederacy in Missouri. Farms belonging to those who could prove their loyalty to the Union wouldn't be touched. It was a cruel punishment. The area surrounding the Town of Kansas was depopulated; homes were burned and fields destroyed. Some of those put off their land settled in the Town of Kansas, and the hardships that the order imposed affected the town's population long after the war.

Artist George Caleb Bingham, who was the state treasurer of Missouri and an ardent Unionist, went to Ewing and pleaded with him to rescind the order, but the officer refused. Bingham told him that if Ewing persisted in carrying out Order No. 11, he would use his talents as an artist to make the general infamous. Ewing went ahead with the forced evacuations of the farms.

Bingham carried out his threat after the war. In 1865 he began his first version of the famous Order No. 11 painting, rendering it on an old board in his Independence studio. He placed a likeness of a stern and forbidding Ewing in the painting. In 1870, when he had his studio in Kansas City above Shannon's Drygoods Store on the southwest corner of Third and Main near the City Market, Bingham painted his final version of the picture on a linen tablecloth he got from the store. Copies of the painting were made and circulated widely throughout the country. These copies were later cited as one of the reasons that Ewing was defeated in his run for a congressional seat in Ohio.

Bingham, known for his paintings depicting life on the frontier, painted portraits of many of the town's early settlers. In 1859 he rendered a portrait of Dr. Benoist Troost, one of the town's earliest physicians. Today this portrait hangs in the Nelson-Atkins Gallery of Art. In 1872 Bingham became the president of the town's first police board. He died in 1879 and is buried in Union Cemetery at 28th and Warwick Trafficway.

The Battle of Westport was the Civil War's largest conflict west of the Mississippi. It was fought from Independence, Missouri, west along the Blue River, then along today's 63rd Street and north on Wornall Road. The turning point of the battle occurred on Sunday, October 23, in present-day Loose Park and the surrounding area.

The battle was the end of the invasion of Missouri started by Major General Sterling Price, in command of 12,000 Confederate troops that he called the Army of Missouri. Price led his troops into Arkansas, and on September 21, 1864, they crossed the border into Missouri. Their objective was to take St. Louis.

When General Thomas Ewing, who was then commander of the Union forces at St. Louis, was alerted to the approaching Southern army, he sent troops to stop them. The two armies met at Pilot Knob, just 80 miles from St. Louis. In the ensuing battle, Price lost 1,500 men. After deciding to take his remaining troops west to capture Jefferson City, he received information that there was a large number of Union troops waiting for him there. So Price changed his strategy, moving his troops west to take West Port and then pushing on to take the Town of Kansas, and then he planned to move northwest to capture the large arsenal at Fort Leavenworth.

On October 10, the Confederate troops occupied Boonville and were joined by over 1,500 new recruits. Price marched his men on to Arrow Rock, and then they battled their way through Lexington. By this time 8,000 Union troops were tailing them, 4,000 were on Price's left flank, and ahead was the Kansas Militia.

At dawn on the morning of October 19, the Army of Missouri attacked Union troops holding the line on the western bank of the Little Blue River, not far from Independence, Missouri. Price's army pushed the Union soldiers into and through Independence with heavy fighting just north of the town's square. By Saturday the 22nd, Union troops, pursued by Confederate forces, had retreated east to the Big Blue River and Bryam's Ford (today's 63rd and Manchester). Fighting spread from the Big Blue River to Missouri's western border and north to Brush Creek. There was fighting all around the John Wornall home, still standing on 61st Terrace, which was used as a hospital for the wounded of both sides.

By Sunday, October 23, Price had moved the majority of his men to the hills south of Brush Creek in the area that today is the Sunset Hill neighborhood. Troops from the Kansas Militia and volunteers from the Town of Kansas were massed on the opposite side of the creek. Price's soldiers had the advantage of protection by the high cliffs that faced the creek. His marksmen, well-hidden in the rocks and brush, pinned down any Union soldier who moved. Price directed his troops from under a large oak tree that stood near 55th and Pennsylvania. Union General Samuel Curtis headquartered in the Harris House Hotel, which stood on the northeast corner of Westport Road and Pennsylvania. He watched the battle from the hotel's roof through binoculars.

The tide of the conflict was turned by one man, not a soldier but a 45-year-old German farmer named George Thoman, who was looking for his horse that had been stolen by Confederate troops from his farm near 55th and Prospect. On the morning of October 22, while he was wandering around searching for the mare, Thoman encountered a Union officer. He told him that he knew of a ravine leading from Brush Creek to the battlefield that would allow troops to get behind the Confederate line without being seen. With an artillery barrage diverting the Rebels, General Curtis himself led his troops up the hidden ravine (today's Rockwell Lane). They broke through the Confederate line just as more Union troops advanced from the west and a battery of Union cannons placed on Wornall Road started a barrage of fire. Foot soldiers and cavalrymen fought hand to hand. The Brush Creek battlefield was soon strewn with bodies. It was estimated that in the continual fighting from Lexington to Independence to the Battle of Westport, there were 3,500 casualties.

Price pulled his remaining troops south, hoping to get to the Arkansas River. As the soldiers retreated, they set fire to dry grass, hoping that the smoke would screen them. Curtis's men, joined by Missouri and Kansas militia and cavalry from Iowa and Colorado, stayed in hot pursuit. There were battles all along Missouri's western border. The Southern casualty rate was high, and a number of soldiers were taken prisoner. Some of those Confederate troops who did get away made it to Texas and crossed over into Mexico. But by the night of October 25, the invasion of Missouri had been defeated.

During the 1870s, legendary figures of the Wild West—Jesse James, Wild Bill Hickok, Wyatt Earp, and others—patronized the gambling halls on Main and Walnut Streets by the Market Square. Every kind of game of chance was played there: poker, keno, faro, roulette, dice, and even cock and dog fights. The area was called "Battle Row" because of the many fist and gun fights there. Several gamblers were killed in duels because they questioned each other's honesty.

In 1873 James Butler "Wild Bill" Hickok, who had fought in the Battle of Westport, was living in town and was a regular faro player at Marble Hall on Main Street. One day Hickok was wearing a pair of fancy ivory-handled revolvers when Chief of Police Tom Speers asked him what he could do with them. Hickok told Speers to look at the "O" in a saloon sign over 100 yards away. Wild Bill fired five shots from each gun. When Speers went to look, all 10 bullets had hit within the inside of the "O." When "Buffalo" Bill Cody came to town, he talked Wild Bill into appearing in Cody's Wild West Show.

Wyatt Earp, who later took part in the famous O.K. Corral face-off, was a frequent visitor to the area. He said in a newspaper interview that those who wore buckskins on the plains dressed up in only the finest linen shirts, the best black broadcloth frock coats, fancy vests, wide-brimmed sombreros or sometimes silk hats, and boots of handsome black calfskin when they were at the Town of Kansas' Market Square.

"Bat" Masterson also lived here for a time. He not only gambled, but liked to attend the annual agricultural fairs east of the town.

Jesse and Frank James both spent time and money in the market area gambling and visiting a relative who managed the Pacific House Hotel at Fourth and Delaware. (The building, much altered, is still there, empty and boarded up.) Using the names Howard or J. T. Jackson, Jesse lived south of Independence Avenue near Eighth and Woodland, and Eighth and Forest. When walking the streets around the Market, he often carried a cane and wore a patch over one eye as a disguise. He was recognized but left alone.

Jesse frequently wrote letters to the publisher and editor of *The Kansas City Times*, John Edwards, who had been a major in the Confederate Army. Edwards not only printed the letters but wrote articles glorifying the James brothers. After Jesse James was killed on April 3, 1882, in St. Joseph, Missouri, by Robert Ford, the *Times* editor published articles portraying Jesse as the Robin Hood of the Midwest. There have been 30 movies made about Jesse James, one of which starred his son. Today the James family farm in Kearney, just north of Kansas City, is a museum open to the public.

Kansas City's first St. Patrick's Day Parade took place on March 17, 1873. There were 200 Irish families in the city, and it was said they all participated in the procession around the City Market area. Every year the parade got bigger. In 1892 St. Patrick's Day was declared a city holiday so that city employees could join in the parade, which included most of the city's police and firemen. There were floats, decorated wagons pulled by horses, and marching bands. It was reported that the parade was a mile long. Today's organizers of Kansas City's downtown parade claim that it is the third largest in the country. St. Pat's parades also take place in several of the city's neighborhoods and in North Kansas City and in many Johnson County communities.

Eugene Field, who was called "The Children's Poet" because he wrote "Wynken, Blynken, and Nod" and the famous "Twinkle, Twinkle Little Star," was managing editor for The Kansas City Times in 1880. He liked to dine at Herman's Restaurant at 809 Main. Mr. Herman said that Field couldn't write unless he was drinking, and he often paid for his liquor with a poem.

Famous Western artist Frederick Remington lived in the Northeast area of Kansas City in the early 1880s. He traveled on horseback from his home to a saloon in the market area that he owned an interest in. It was said that Remington was handy with his fists and drank so much that the saloon went broke. He later moved West.

On May 11, 1886, a tornado swept through Kansas City. It moved through the middle of town, taking off the top of the County Courthouse at Second and Main. One person was killed in the court-house, a man

The 1886 tornado weakened the bell tower on top of Lathrop School and sent it tumbling down into the building, killing 15 children.

who had gotten out as the tornado approached but went back in to get his umbrella. The force of the wind also caused the bell tower on the Lathrop School at Ninth and Broadway to crash into the school, collapsing the third and second floors into the basement and burying children in the debris. Fifteen students were killed and 18 severely injured. After this tragedy, bell towers were no longer permitted on top of schools. The winds also caused destruction of homes and businesses in the eastern part of the city, where many residents were killed.

Lamon Vernon Harkness, at the time one of the richest men in America, in 1888 built a house at 3125 Troost, an area called "Millionaire's Row." Harkness inherited his fortune from his father, who was a friend of John D. Rockefeller and a partner in starting Standard Oil. It is not known for sure what brought the younger Harkness to town. He had houses all over the world, never spending a great deal of time in one place because he said that fortune hunters were always annoying him. He didn't spend much time here either, and few knew him. In 1891 he moved for good to Lexington, Kentucky, where he had an extensive horse breeding farm outlined by 40 miles of fence.

Ragtime composer Scott Joplin completed his "Original Rag" while living in Sedalia, Missouri. He tried to get it published there but was turned down. Joplin came to Kansas City in 1897 and struck a deal with a publisher here. He sold his rights to the music before it was published. When it was printed, Joplin's name did not appear on the work, and the copyright was registered under the arranger's name. Joplin went back to Sedalia, wrote the "Maple Leaf Rag" and published it there under his name, and thus changed the direction of modern music.

The city's first Convention Hall opened February 22, 1899. William Rockhill Nelson, owner and publisher of *The Kansas City Star*, started writing articles in his newspaper in 1893 that pushed for the construction of a hall big enough for large exhibits, concerts, and conventions. Interest in the project began to grow. In 1897, stock was issued to finance construction of the building. Eventually it was erected, at a cost of $225,000, from Central to Wyandotte, and from 12th to 13th streets (where The BarneyAllis Plaza is today).

The hall opened in the spring of 1899 to the music of two concerts by "March King" John Phillip Sousa's band. That evening there was a gala ball. The Democratic National Convention was booked for the next

People came from all over the city to view the ruins of their new Convention Hall.

year's Fourth of July. But it was what happened at Convention Hall on April 4, 1900, and its consequences that are remembered today.

That evening a fire broke out and completely destroyed the new hall as well as several adjacent buildings. As the word spread, the mayor received a telegram from the Democratic Committee, who wanted to know if the town could still host their convention. Mayor James Reed replied that the hall would be ready by July, and it was. The endeavor was called "The Ninety Day Miracle."

Money to rebuild was raised immediately. Steel companies were contacted and pledged their cooperation in getting new steel girders made and shipped quickly. Railroads promised to give the freight trains carrying the steel priority on the tracks to Kansas City. The city's labor unions urged their skilled laborers—masons, carpenters, and steel workers—to work around the clock. The whole town rallied behind getting the new Convention Hall done by July 4. The effort was named "The Kansas City Spirit."

Work continued right up to the morning of July 4, and the Democratic Committee was pleased with the new hall. They chose William Jennings Bryan as their presidential candidate, the same man who had been defeated four years earlier. And it happened again—Republican

William McKinley won the election. Bryan was nominated by his party a third time in 1908 and lost to William Howard Taft.

An investigation in February 1910 by a grand jury found that Dr. Bennett Clark Hyde should be tried for the murder of Thomas Swope, the man who gave Kansas City 1,346 acres of land for a park that was named after him. Swope was a shy, reclusive fellow who had made millions buying real estate in downtown and reselling it at great profits.

In 1905, Hyde eloped with the oldest daughter of Thomas Swope's deceased brother, Logan. His brother's widow, Margaret, did not approve of Hyde because he was known to have had affairs with women and to have taken money from them. After the marriage, the wealthy Thomas Swope gave the couple $10,000 to buy a house and got Dr. Hyde appointed to the staff of City Hospital (later General Hospital).

Swope, in his eighties, lived in his sister-in-law's mansion in Independence along with several of her children and her financial advisor and Thomas Swope's executor, elderly J. Moss Hunton. On October 1, Dr. Hyde took over as physician for Hunton and, over the previous physician's objections, prescribed bleeding to relieve the old man's arterial pressure. Hyde took two quarts of blood and the patient died immediately. A nurse later reported that just after Mr. Hunton died, the doctor had asked her to pressure Thomas Swope to make him the executor of Swope's $3.5 million estate.

Three days later, Dr. Hyde gave the nurse a "digestive" capsule for Mr. Swope, who after taking it died. Later the 30-year-old son of Mrs. Swope died after the doctor administered a fever capsule. In the next several months, 10 cases of typhoid struck the family and household staff. Everyone but the Hydes were ill. Dr. Hyde blamed it on the water from the cistern and brought several bottles of distilled water to the house, putting them in the icebox. Even then, when one of the servants drank that water, she became ill.

When Mrs. Swope's daughter Sarah became ill, Dr. Hyde gave her nurse a capsule to give to her, but the nurse did not and the girl recovered. When Mrs. Swope herself became ill, her nurse saw Dr. Hyde substitute one of his capsules for those that the patient's personal physician had left. Mrs. Swope took one and immediately had a seizure, similar to those that preceded the deaths of her brother-in-law and her son. However, she recovered. After hearing from the nurse that she had taken a capsule substituted by Hyde, Mrs. Swope told the servants to show him out of the house and not let him return.

Just as Hyde was leaving, Mrs. Swope's son Tom came around the corner and observed the doctor dropping something on the sidewalk and grinding it underfoot as he hurried away. After searching to see what had been dropped, Swope found fragments of a capsule. He had worked in a mill that used cyanide to test ore and he recognized that the fragmented capsule had the same odor as cyanide. He brought the substance to a pharmacist who confirmed his suspicions.

Witnesses at the trial testified that Hyde had purchased capsules of potassium cyanide at a drugstore, where he told the druggist he was going to use it to get rid of insects. The druggist also testified that Hyde bought a box of digestive capsules that looked similar to the cyanide pills. Also, colleagues at the hospital testified that prior to the deaths, Hyde purchased over 200 test tubes and secured cultures containing typhoid germs, which he planted in the tubes, telling his colleagues that he was setting up a laboratory to study bacteria,

The grand jury handed down 11 indictments against Hyde that included trying to infect the whole Swope household with typhoid. But the doctor was tried only for the murder of Thomas Swope, whose body had been exhumed and autopsied, showing evidence of enough cyanide to kill him.

It was pointed out at the trial that Thomas Swope's $3.5 million estate was left to his sister-in-law and her family—which meant that Hyde's wife would benefit from the deaths of her mother, brothers, and sisters. Frances Swope Hyde testified on her husband's behalf, saying she had absolute confidence that he did not do any of the things he was accused of. Her mother also testified. Facing her daughter, Margaret Swope told of all that she and others had observed and blamed the doctor for the murder of Thomas Swope.

The evidence convinced the jury of Hyde's guilt and they recommended life imprisonment. But the doctor appealed, and the Supreme Court reversed the decision, citing that murder was never proven. Hyde was tried two more times: one was declared a mistrial because a bored juror crawled over a transom and escaped from the courthouse, and the other ended in a hung jury.

The Swope family spent over a quarter of a million dollars trying to convict Hyde, who nonetheless continued to practice medicine. They dropped the case. Frances divorced him in 1920, saying that his temper made her fear for her life and those of her children. Hyde died in 1934.

Was the doctor a serial killer who murdered three people and tried to do in eight more? The question will never be answered.

Lillian Russell, who was the leading actress of the Broadway stage for almost 40 years, was appearing at the Shubert Theater at 10th and Baltimore in 1913. As she left the Baltimore Hotel, just a block south of the theater, a thief grabbed her purse and ran. Russell, 52 at the time, chased him down and beat him to the ground with her umbrella. She kept hitting him until a policeman came to take him to jail.

In 1914, owners of the Florida Fruit Farm Company, located in Kansas City, were put on trial by the federal government because they sold Florida swampland west of Lake Okeechobee to over 1,000 farmers in the Midwest as ideal for fruit farms. Company representatives had gone to small towns and posted notices about cheap land in Florida that was excellent for growing fruit. Farmers signed up and made a down payment to buy the land, which they were not told was under water most of the time. The company principals, because they mailed the exact locations of the land to the buyers along with a bill for the money owed, were arrested for mail fraud.

One hundred of the victimized farmers came to town to testify at the trial, heard in the Federal Courthouse downtown. The owners of the company were found guilty. They appealed and were found guilty again in 1916 and sent to prison.

Evangelist Billy Sunday came to town in 1916 to conduct seven weeks of revival meetings. Before becoming a preacher he had played for three major league baseball clubs. He was on the Chicago White Stockings team in 1886 when they played the Kansas City Cowboys. Sunday used baseball slang, exaggerated body movements, and flamboyant gestures to put his sermons across. The newspaper printed drawings of some of his more colorful moves. (It was said that writer Sinclair Lewis used him as the model for the preacher in Elmer Gantry.)

Billy Sunday also developed a highly successful promotion team that went before him to spread his name across the country. This PR made him the most popular evangelist of his time. Six months before he came to Kansas City, the city's newspapers began printing articles about the revival. Fifty churchmen, members of the Ministerial Alliance, gathered together and rehearsed a choir of 2,000 singers, the largest ever organized in the city, to appear every night of the revival.

The huge tabernacle built for Sunday at Independence Avenue and Lydia, the former ballfield site, was said to have a seating capacity of 12,000 and standing room for 4,000 more. (Nothing remains of the building today.) The evangelist's "campaign for souls" began April 24, 1916. At the first meeting, the crowd was estimated at 20,000, mostly women. Large throngs continued to attend throughout the seven-week revival.

Ministers from various churches supported the revivals; some appeared at the meetings before the evangelist came on to warm up the crowd. Billy Sunday's message that "Kansas City is the most pleasure mad city I have ever visited" not only attracted large audiences, but filled the collection plates passed among the faithful at the meetings.

Not every minister was taken with Sunday. One said "Billy Sunday is typical of religious teachers who no longer appeal to the intelligence. They appeal to emotions and fear . . . people pay for it. The men who take the rake off, particularly those who take in large quantities, like Billy Sunday, are too smooth at the game of stirring up the emotions to be detected by the ordinary emotional creature."

After seven weeks of "hell fire and damnation," Sunday moved on to the next town.

A labor strike in Kansas City during the last of March in 1918 involved almost 40,000 workers and effectively shut down the city. It started in January when 10 laundry drivers stopped working because the laundry owners wouldn't pay them a set weekly salary instead of by the laundry bundle they picked up and delivered. The strike continued, and soon laundry workers across the city organized a union, both to get better pay and to see the enforcement of the Missouri law covering working conditions and how many hours women could work. They made a proposal to the laundry owners and when they rejected the union's demands, strikers overturned and burned company wagons carrying laundry and stoned laundry buildings. Their actions drew gunfire, killing one man.

On March 15, 500 union delegates representing the 150 unions in town met at the Labor Temple building at 14th and Woodland and voted to call a general strike on March 27 in sympathy with the laundry workers. It was agreed that workers would not strike those companies that had government contracts to supply materials for soldiers fighting the First World War in Europe. Unless the laundry strike was settled, members of the building trades as well as bartenders, barbers, butchers, restaurant and hotel employees, and retail store workers would walk off their jobs in 12 days. The laundry owners would not settle.

The strike was called. On the morning of March 27, mobs of workers took to the streets, going in and out of stores, hotels, and restaurants, asking workers to leave their jobs and join them. By the end of the day, all major restaurants and hotels had closed because they had no workers. Construction workers walked off their jobs, and most downtown businesses closed. At 1:30 p.m. the next day, 1,600 members of the streetcar workers abandoned their cars and joined the strike. People were stranded with no way to get home. Family dinner tables didn't have bread or meat because bakeries and butcher shops were closed. Large numbers of strikers roamed the streets, threatening workers who hadn't walked away from their jobs. The local police couldn't handle the mobs, so the mayor called out the National Guard to patrol the streets and maintain order.

City leaders feared mass violence, and worried that if the strike lasted too long, the mayor and city council election scheduled the next week would be affected. The mayor telegraphed the national president of the Street and Electric Railway Employees union in Detroit, asking him to come to town and try to convince local labor leaders to call off the strike.

He came on the next train and sat down with owners and local union leaders. An agreement was reached April 2 and people went back to work immediately. The laundry owners increased their women workers' salaries, from $8 to $9 a week. As they worked 45 hours a week, this guaranteed them a wage of 20 cents an hour. And the laundry drivers who started it all? They would be rehired but were still to be paid by the bundle. What it cost the city when 40,000 walked off of their jobs for a week is not known.

Eighteen-year-old Ernest Hemingway got his first writing job at *The Kansas City Star* in 1917 as a reporter covering the police station and General Hospital. He lived with a friend at 35th and Agnes. Hemingway left Kansas City in 1918 to become an ambulance driver in France, where he was severely wounded during the last days of World War I.

The writer and his wife returned to the Kansas City area in 1927. While living in a relative's house in Mission Hills, Kansas, Hemingway finished *A Farewell to Arms*, the novel based on his experiences in the war. His two sons, Patrick and Gregory, were born at Research Hospital during this time. He returned to Kansas City in 1931 and lived for a time at the Riviera Apartments, across Brush Creek from The Plaza.

Another famous novelist, Sinclair Lewis, spent a month in Kansas City during 1926 while researching his novel, *Elmer Gantry*. Lewis took a suite of rooms at the Ambassador Hotel at 35th and Broadway, where he held weekly luncheons with the city's leading clergymen as guests. He challenged them with such questions as how they could preach on subjects they didn't believe. He attended various church meetings, Bible classes, and area revivals and even gave a sermon at a church on Linwood Boulevard. While here, Lewis turned down the Pulitzer Prize for *Arrowsmith*.

By the time he left Kansas City, Lewis had his idea for the novel he had referred to as "The Preacher" book. He wrote it that summer on a farm in Minnesota. When *Elmer Gantry* was published the next year, its theme of religious hypocrisy and bigotry in the Midwest caused a stir throughout the country. Several libraries refused to have the book on their shelves. In Kansas City, ministers who had attended Lewis's luncheons were busy denying that they were Gantry while some took credit for various ideas in the book.

In his later years, Lewis seized every opportunity to warn the country that religious fundamentalists and fanatics were seeking to take over the government.

Queen Marie of Romania came to Kansas City on November 11, 1926, to take part in the dedication of the Liberty Memorial. Marie was the daughter of Britain's Queen Victoria. Her work with the Red Cross on the battlefields during the First World War had made her an international heroine. She wrote weekly newspaper columns that appeared in this country and won her many fans.

Marie and two of her children, Prince Nicholas and Princess Ileana, arrived at Union Station in their special train, painted royal blue. One hundred fifty thousand people lined the streets to cheer as she drove to the Hotel Muehlebach and then to the Liberty Memorial for the dedication. The royal family was here only six hours, but Her Majesty was the honored guest that evening at a concert in the American Royal building. The concert's proceeds were to be spent for an outdoor theater. The $7,000 raised was kept in an account and in 1950 was contributed to the building of Starlight Theatre.

On the morning of June 17, 1933, Frank Nash, an escapee from Leavenworth Prison who had been apprehended in Hot Springs, Arkansas, was taken by train to Kansas City's Union Station. He was accompanied by two special Justice Department agents (they were not called FBI then) and an Oklahoma chief of police. Outside of the station two more special agents and two Kansas City detectives were waiting with a car to take Nash to the federal prison at Leavenworth.

Also outside in a car, however, were three men armed with machine guns and pistols. It is believed that "Pretty Boy" Floyd was one of them. As Nash and his escorts came out of the station and moved toward the car where the other detectives were waiting, the three gangsters moved toward them with guns raised. The Kansas City detective started shooting. Soon shots were coming from every angle. The barrage lasted five minutes, leaving four of the officers dead and four wounded. Nash, too, was dead, supposedly killed by shots from the criminals' guns. The gangsters got away. The shoot-out became known as "The Union Station Massacre."

"Pretty Boy" Floyd was a hero to some farmers in the Midwest because he robbed banks. During the Depression, banks foreclosed on farms and put farmers off their land because they couldn't pay their mortgages. Some farmers thought Floyd, like Jesse James, was a Robin Hood figure. Sometimes "Pretty Boy" gave money to those down on their luck, and they hid him when he was on the run.

Floyd had been in trouble since he was 18 years old. He had been arrested and put in prison several times for holdups and stealing. When he got out of jail, he continued to commit robberies. He was caught and sentenced to 15 years in jail, but then he leaped from the speeding train that was taking him to prison and escaped. He never again was taken into custody. Floyd started using a machine gun in his robberies, often shooting at the first sight of a policeman. From 1931 to 1932 he and his band pulled over 50 holdups and it is thought that he killed five or six men himself, four of whom were policemen.

"Pretty Boy" lived Kansas City on and off during 1931 and 1932. Although never a part of organized crime, many thought that Floyd was contracted by crime bosses to rescue Frank Nash. After the massacre, manhunts were conducted for the slayers, especially Floyd. Over the next year he was seen but not apprehended.

By late October 1934, Floyd was in Ohio, robbing banks as usual. Wellsville police received a tip that robbery suspects were camping near their town by a river. The chief and two officers went to investigate and found two men wrapped in blankets. As they approached, one of the men drew a gun and started firing; the other ran into the woods. Two of the policemen were hit. One robber was caught and said that the other who got away was Floyd.

Roadblocks were set up. On October 22, Floyd, who had been hiding in the woods, approached a farmhouse and told the owner, who didn't recognize him, that he had gotten lost while hunting. He asked for some food and to see a newspaper. A farmer in the next field had seen Floyd come out of the woods and recognized him. He called the local police, who then alerted federal agents.

Floyd talked the owner's son into giving him a ride to the next town. As their car started to move out of the farmyard, two cars came speeding down the main road and pulled into the yard. Floyd jumped from the car and ran toward the woods with his pistol in his hand. The police and federal agents got out of their cars and followed. Nine officers armed with various pistols and rifles began shooting at Floyd as he ran across the field. The fugitive went down bleeding from several bullet holes. He was still conscious when the lawmen reached him. They asked if he was "Pretty Boy" Floyd. He answered, "I am Charles Arthur Floyd," and died.

Several movie actors who were either born here or spent part of their early lives here worked together at the Metro-Goldwyn-Mayer film studios. They were MGM's biggest stars in the 1930s and 1940s.

Clark Gable was 19 when he came to Kansas City in 1920. Hired by a local traveling acting company, his job included putting up tents, playing the French horn in the orchestra, walking around town in a clown costume selling tickets, and occasionally playing small parts, which according to biographers he did not do well.

In 1916 Spencer Tracy, who made San Francisco, Test Pilot, and Boom Town with Clark Gable, spent six months in town as a student at Rockhurst High School, then located at 52nd and Troost. Years later he remembered going to Electric Park and seeing his first professional plays at the Shubert Theater downtown.

Jean Harlow was born March 3, 1911, in Kansas City and christened Harlean Carpenter. Her father was a dentist and her mother, Jean, had aspirations to become an actress. Harlean attended Barstow School, then located on Westport Road. When she was 10 her parents divorced and her mother took her to Hollywood, California. Mrs. Carpenter didn't get into the movies, but a teenage Harlean, accompanying a friend to a movie lot, was noticed and asked to appear in small roles. Taking her mother's first name and maiden name, she became Jean Harlow. Howard Hughes, needing an unknown for his film Hell's Angels, made her a star. At MGM she made three movies with Spencer Tracy, appeared with Wallace Beery in three films, and co-starred with Clark Gable (her good friend) in five films. She died in 1937 at the age of 26 while making Saratoga with Gable.

At the time of Harlow's death she was engaged to fellow MGM actor William Powell, who had appeared with her in Reckless in 1934 and Libeled Lady in 1936. Powell, born in Kansas City in 1892, attended Central High School, where he was a cheerleader. Despite his father's objections, the young man took up acting, went to New York, and appeared on the Broadway stage. He is most remembered for his MGM Thin Man film series.

Another MGM actor born here was Wallace Beery, whose father was a member of Kansas City's police force for 27 years. The Beerys lived near 12th and The Paseo. At 16, Wallace ran away to join the circus. His first job on Broadway was playing in the chorus dressed as a girl. By 1913 he was appearing in the silent Keystone Cops comedy films. His brother, Noah, also an actor, usually played villain roles. Wallace signed on with MGM in the 1920s and by the 1930s his films were some of the top moneymakers. Besides his films with Gable and Harlow, he also appeared in Grand Hotel with Joan Crawford.

Joan Crawford was born Lucille le Sueur in 1904 in Oklahoma. When her mother married her second husband, Lucille became Billie Cassin. At age five, she started taking dancing lessons. Her mother divorced again and moved to Kansas City. Billie was enrolled in St. Agnes Academy, a private girls' school in the Northeast section of town. After high school she worked as a sales clerk at Emery, Bird, Thayer department store. Billie won trophies in dance contests at Electric Park. She moved first to Chicago, then New York to dance in various nightclubs. An MGM talent scout saw her perform in New York and arranged a screen test, and she became Joan Crawford. Four years later she was one of MGM's biggest stars.

Although Ruth Warrick did not work at MGM, her first movie role will be remembered forever. She was born in Kansas City, graduated from Westport High School, and was a local beauty contest winner. While vacationing in New York, by chance she met Orson Wells at a party. He chose her to portray his wife in the film classic Citizen Kane. For over 20 years Ruth Warrick played the role of Phoebe Snow on the television soap opera "All My Children."

Sally Rand fan-danced her way to fame. Born Billie Beck in 1904 in the Ozarks, Sally's family moved to Kansas City when she was four years old. Like William Powell, she also attended Central High School. Sally said she took her stage name from the Rand McNally atlas. At 18

Sally Rand, more or less, in costume.

she joined a vaudeville show and began touring the country. While appearing in Los Angeles, Max Sennett, director of the Keystone Cops silent movie comedies, saw her and gave her a role diving from a 35-foot tower into a tank of water. She made several silent movies for Cecil B. deMille, the director of epic Bible films. When sound came to the movies, her voice killed her film career. She then became an exotic dancer in burlesque.

Sally's fan dance was the sensation of the 1933 Chicago World's Fair. She continued to dance, with only fans to cover her body, for many years, making several appearances in her hometown. Sally's last fan dance here took place in 1978 at age 74 for the benefit of the Historic Kansas City Foundation. She died in 1979.

Between 1942 and 1945 there were two prisoner of war camps near Kansas City. Six hundred German POWs captured in Africa, members of Field Marshal Erwin Rommel's Afrika Korps, were sent to Liberty, Missouri, where the Army built barracks for them on a turkey farm. The camp was surrounded by a 10-foot barbed wire fence with guard tower and patrolled by 50 military policemen from Fort Leavenworth. The prisoners not only worked on potato farms around Liberty but were transported to Kansas City to work in a box factory and in the stockyards.

Italian POWs, also from the African campaign, were housed in horse stalls at the old Riverside Race Track. The prisoners were bused to the Quartermaster Depot at Independence Avenue and Hardesty, where the personal effects of American soldiers killed in action were sent. The Italian POWS helped to package these materials so they could be shipped to the soldiers' families. Some of the Italian prisoners were allowed to visit families in the city's Italian community. After the war ended, many of them didn't want to go back to Italy. The Catholic dioceses sponsored their stay in the city and got them jobs.

A hideous crime happened in Kansas City on September 28, 1953. That morning, a woman appeared at an exclusive Kansas City Catholic school where six-year-old Bobby Greenlease was a student and told one of the nuns that the child's mother had suffered a heart attack. She said that she was Bobby's aunt and had been sent to get the boy because his mother was asking for him. The nun got the child from his classroom, and Bobby walked toward the woman as if he knew her. Holding the boy's hand, they got into a cab. That was the last time Bobby Greenlease was seen alive. Once the kidnapping became known, the whole city was held in fear—for the little boy taken and for the safety of other children.

After the kidnappers were caught, the woman, Bonnie Heady, confessed that in the cab she had asked little Bobby questions about his dogs and his life at home so that she could use the information in the ransom notes and phone calls to his family.

Her accomplice, Carl Austin Hall, was waiting in a station-wagon at the Katz Drug Store at Main and Westport Road. Bonnie and the boy got in and Hall drove to a field near Lenexa, Kansas, where he shot Bobby in the head, wrapped his body in a plastic sheet, and stuffed him into the back of the car. Then the couple drove to St. Joseph, Missouri, where Bonnie lived, dug a hole in her backyard, and buried Bobby's body. They wrote a ransom note asking for $600,000 and went to the post office to send it special delivery. While they were out, they bought chrysanthemums to plant over Bobby's grave.

An hour after Bobby had been taken from the school, one of the nuns called his home asking how Mrs. Greenlease was. It was apparent that the boy had been kidnapped and the police were called.

In addition to owning the Cadillac dealership in Kansas City, the boy's father, Robert Greenlease, also owned or was a partner in several dealerships throughout the Midwest. He was reported to be one of the 10 most wealthy men in Kansas City. He was older than his wife and not in good health. Two of his friends volunteered to deal with the kidnappers. The ransom note was received that afternoon, stating that the ransom of $600,000 was to be paid in $20s and $10s from 12 Federal Reserve districts. The note said that when the money was ready, an ad reading "Will meet you in Chicago" was to be run in the classifieds of *The Kansas City Star*.

The next morning, Mr. Greenlease went to the Commerce Trust Bank and asked for the money in the denominations and districts requested. He then placed the ad. That afternoon another note arrived at the Greenlease home requesting that the money be put in an Army duffel bag. Enclosed in the letter was a cross that Bobby had worn.

The kidnappers called the house, 15 times in all, and often Mrs. Greenlease answered. She was always reassured that Bobby was alive and would be returned. They cruelly told her lies about what the boy was eating and doing. The duffel bag containing the $600,000 was delivered by Commerce Bank to the Greenlease home. Beforehand, bank employees copied down the bill's serial number.

If Heady and Hall had been as inept at taking the boy as they were at following their own directions regarding the ransom, the kidnapping would have never succeeded. The money was left exactly where they told the Greenleases to have their friends leave the duffel bag. The kidnappers looked in the wrong place and called the house to say it hadn't been delivered. The friends, fearing that someone else would pick up the bag, returned to the spot, retrieved the money, and went back to the house to wait for another call.

On Sunday, October 4, there were two more phone calls to the Greenlease house with new directions. The duffel bag was to be left that afternoon at a spot just off of Highway 40. The caller said that after the money was received, Bobby could be picked up in 24 hours at the Western Union office in Pittsburg, Kansas. Mr. Greenlease's two friends dropped off the money and then drove to Pittsburg to wait. After two days, they returned to Kansas City on October 7, knowing it was unlikely Bobby would be coming back. As soon as they got back they received a call from the St. Louis police, telling them that two people had confessed to kidnapping Bobby and killing him. It was up to the friends to tell the Greenleases.

After Hall and Heady picked up the duffel bag, they drove in a rented car to St. Louis, where Hall bought a footlocker and dumped the money into it. They went to several bars, had many drinks, and started to argue about what to do with the money. They ditched the car they had rented in St. Joseph and checked into a hotel. Bonnie passed out and Hall took the money and left her, never to return.

He hired cabs, bought a car, stayed at various motels, took up with a cab driver and a prostitute, and flashed a fist full of money. He gave the driver $2,500 to buy him a suit and liquor. While he was asleep, the prostitute looked into the footlocker and saw the money. She told the cab driver when he returned what she had seen and left. The driver, an ex-convict, became concerned that he might be implicated in whatever Hall had done. He called someone he knew on the St. Louis police force and brought them to Hall's hotel room.

The police found the footlocker full of money and took Hall to jail. Under questioning, he implicated Heady, but said that a third person had planned the kidnapping, although he couldn't tell them much about who or where he was. Finally, on the morning of October 7, he told them that Bobby was buried in Heady's backyard.

Little Bobby Greenlease's body was dug up and taken to Kansas

City. On October 9, a funeral mass was said for him at St. Agnes Church and Bobby was buried in consecrated ground.

Justice moved much more swiftly then. The kidnappers were tried on November 16, not quite two months after the crime. It took three days to find them guilty and they were executed a month later. When the police counted the money in the footlocker, there was only $300,000. Hall didn't know where the other $300,000 had gone, and it was never found.

In 1953, in order to build the Sixth Street Trafficway that connects with I-70 east and west just north of Kansas City's downtown, 125 buildings were demolished. Most of them were built in the 1870s, '80s, and '90s. Destroying these buildings erased a great deal of the town's early history.

On September 17, 1964, the Beatles came to perform in Kansas City's Municipal Stadium. Charles O. Finley, owner of the Kansas City Athletics, paid them $150,000 for a 30-minute performance to benefit Children's Mercy Hospital. The stadium was soon sold out. Police Chief Clarence Kelley assigned 350 policemen to handle the crowd, expected to be more than 18,000. The chief was quoted as saying that he would rather see an invasion from Mars than have to contend with the mass hysteria of Beatles fans. A line of policemen were to stand in front of the stage and form a barricade against their enthusiastic, adoring fans. The stadium was packed for the performance, and the concert came off without a hitch.

The Beatles spent the night in the Hotel Muehlebach's Terrace Penthouse. The next morning they left for Dallas. The hotel's switchboard was overloaded with calls from fans offering to buy anything the group had touched. The Muehlebach sold 16 sheets and 8 pillowcases for $750. Someone offered to buy a bathtub that any of the Beatles had bathed in, but the hotel wouldn't go that far.

Pieces of the saffron-colored nylon fabric that the artist Christo used to cover the walks at Loose Park in October 1978 were also sold to the public. The Contemporary Art Society of the Nelson Gallery invited Christo to consider Kansas City as a location for one of his projects. Wanting to do a large wrapped walkway for almost 10 years, the artist came here in 1977 and found Loose Park ideal for the project.

Christo prepared a proposal for the Kansas City Parks Department, assuming all of the costs and liability for the project. The Art Society lobbied the city and the project was approved.

Wrapping the sidewalks began on October 2. Eighty-four paid workers and volunteers began to install the 136,268 square feet of golden cloth that would cover 104,836 square feet of the park's walks and jogging paths. Workers hammered in steel spikes driven through brass grommets in the cloth to hold the work in place.

The process of wrapping the walks became a show in itself. Hundred of people flocked to the park to see what was going on. The installation took only two days. "Wrapped Walk Ways" lasted from October 4 through October 16. Even though it rained and even hailed during the two weeks, people came to Loose Park to walk, run, and even dance on the golden walks. Then it was over; the fabric was taken up and given to the Parks Department, which offered pieces for sale.

Years from now, when descendents find a square piece of golden material among a relative's prized treasures, they may wonder what it was for. It was for joy.

Loose Park's walks were wrapped in gold in 1978.

Photo courtesy of Bob Barrett

FOR THE SPORT OF IT

Who knows when people started throwing around a rock or chasing each other playing tag. When did a game become a sport? Professional athletic events that started in Kansas City before the 20th century are still attracting fans today.

Civil War troops of both sides played baseball to relieve stress and tension between battles. After the war, soldiers brought the game back home with them. In 1866, a year after the Civil War ended, Kansas City organized its first baseball team, the Antelopes. The team played the Hope Club, a local scrub team, on a field at 14th Street between Oak and McGee. At the end of the season, the Antelopes met the Frontier Club of Leavenworth, Kansas, in a playoff game. The Antelopes won 47 to 27.

In 1884, the Cowboys, Kansas City's first professional baseball team, was in the eight-team Union Association. They played on a field called Athletic Park, in Cook's pasture near Summit and Southwest Boulevard. Kansas City offered its first ladies day and rainchecks that year. The team finished sixth. The Union Association lasted only one season. The next year the Cowboys were in the Western Association, but that league folded before the season was over. By 1886 the Cowboys had

The Cowboys baseball team in 1886.

switched to the National League and played their games in the city's new League Park, situated on the south side of Independence Avenue at Lydia. The players called the field "The Hole" because when Independence Avenue was graded, dirt was pushed high along the edge of the street, making a mound along the field's perimeter. After a rain the park became a pond. It rained the day before the opening day of the 1886 season and the game had to be postponed until the field could dry out. The next day the Cowboys beat the Chicago White Stockings in a game that went 13 innings.

During the 1888 season, fans began calling the baseball team "The Blues" because they wore blue uniforms. By 1889 the Western League was operating again, and in 1890 the Blues won the league pennant in the final game of the series against Indianapolis. It was the first baseball pennant for Kansas City and the first year the team cleared a profit.

Over the next two decades, professional baseball was played in Exposition Park, west of 15th at Montgall, Sportsman's Park at 17th and Indiana, Association Park at 20th and Olive, and Gorden and Koppel stadium at 48th and Tracy.

Kansas City had two teams in 1902: the Western League's Blue Stockings and The Blues, who played in the American League, at that time not a major league. In 1915 there were again two teams. The Blues played at Association Park and the Packers, of the Federal League, played at 48th and Tracy.

Young brewery owner George Muehlebach started attending Blues games at Association Park. He built the Muehlebach Hotel at 11th and Baltimore in 1915, and that same year he bought a small amount of Blues stock. By 1917 Muehlebach owned controlling interest in the team. In 1923 he built a ballpark for his team at 22nd and Brooklyn. The Blues had a winning streak that year and fans packed the stadium. The Blues beat Baltimore to win the Little World Series in 1923 and set a minor league attendance record of 430,000 for the year. The Blues won the series again in 1929.

But by 1930 the fans seemed to lose interest in the team. Ticket sales dropped lower than any other minor league team. Muehlebach installed lights at the stadium and tried night baseball. Although there was some increase in ticket sales, it didn't justify the cost of lighting the field.

At the end of the 1932 season, Muehlebach sold the Blues and his stadium to a partnership that included the radio and movie comedian

Muehlebach Stadium at 22nd and Brooklyn, the home of the Blues and later the Kansas City Athletics. The Kansas City Chiefs and the Royals played here until 1972. Today the land is used for a municipal garden.

Joe E. Brown. In the summer of 1937 the team and the stadium were sold to the New York Yankees for $230,000, to be used as a minor league farm team. Many big league players started out with this team: Yogi Berra, Mickey Mantle, and Hank Bauer, to name a few.

There was another professional winning baseball team in Kansas City during this time. This team won more championship games than any other in the city's sports history. When these athletes played their home games in the Blues' stadium, crowds filled the grandstand, even while the Blues were having a hard time selling tickets. The team was the Kansas City Monarchs, and from 1920 until 1955 they dominated the Negro baseball leagues.

It took public television's special on the history of baseball in 1994 to tell the Monarchs' story to the nation. Because of segregation during the time they played, the team got little coverage in major newspapers. *The Kansas City Call,* the city's Negro newspaper with a circulation of over 25,000 in the 1920s, was distributed throughout the Southwest. *The Call* kept black communities informed about the Monarchs. The team was not only the pride of Kansas City's black community but of blacks in every city in which they played.

The first national league for Negro baseball clubs came out of a meeting of black baseball owners and sportswriters held at the Paseo YMCA in 1920. J.L. Wilkinson, who earlier had a team called "The All-Nations" because the players were of different races and nationalities, put together the Kansas City Monarchs team that same year. Wilkinson, who was white, was respected by his players and members of the black community. He would own the Monarchs for over 28 years.

The Monarchs won nine league pennants and were the first black world champions. In 1921 they challenged the Kansas City Blues to a championship game at Blues Stadium. The Monarchs won three out of the five games. (For the Blues game, the stadium was segregated with "Whites Only" signs on seating sections.) When Babe Ruth came through town with his Traveling All Stars in 1922, the team lost both of their games to the Monarchs. In the 1920s and 1930s the Monarchs were regarded as equal to any major league team. The Monarchs won the first Negro World Series in 1924 and then won five more times in the next 10 years.

The Monarchs were the first to light ballfields for night games. In 1929 Wilkinson had a portable lighting system built. Poles that could be extended to a height of 50 feet and support six floodlights were powered

The Kansas City Monarchs were one of the best baseball teams in the nation during the 1920s, '30s, and '40s

by a generator that was mounted on truck beds. The trucks were placed outside of the foul lines. The system cost over $50,000, but the lights sold tickets to night games.

During the Depression, when ticket sales went down in Kansas City, the team took to barnstorming small towns, challenging local teams to earn money. They traveled in their own bus to 18 states. It wasn't unusual for them to play one game in the afternoon, then drive to the next town to play another game under lights that evening. The Monarchs played anywhere from 80 to 150 games a season.

Buck O'Neil had the longest tenure with the Monarchs. He came from Sarasota, Florida, in 1938 to play for the team and managed the Monarchs from 1949 until 1955. For a time, O'Neil was a scout for the Chicago Cubs and later for the Royals. He still lives in Kansas City, and at age 80 was one of the narrators of the *History of Baseball* series on public television.

"Satchel" Leroy Paige has been called one of the greatest pitchers in baseball history. He played for touring Negro teams and teams in minor Negro leagues for 30 years. There is little doubt that if he had been allowed to play in the major leagues he would have been recognized as one of baseball's greatest players. Paige started playing professional baseball with the Chattanooga Black Lookouts and joined the Monarchs' traveling farm team in 1939. He liked to jump from club to club, pitching for whichever paid the most money. However, he is listed on the Monarchs roster from 1941 until 1947.

The Cleveland Indians hired Paige in 1948. He helped the team win the American League pennant that year. Later he pitched for the St. Louis Browns, and in 1965, when he was nearly 60 (no one knew his true age), Charles Finley hired him to pitch three innings for the Kansas City Athletics. He was the first Negro baseball player to be named to the Baseball Hall of Fame. Paige died on June 8, 1982, and is buried in Forest Hill Cemetery.

When Jackie Robinson, who had played for the Monarchs in 1945, was hired by the Brooklyn Dodgers in 1947, he broke the color barrier in the major leagues. This started the decline of the Negro leagues, who soon lost their best players and their fans to the majors.

Wilkinson sold the Monarchs in 1948. The team carried on for 16 more years, mostly barnstorming in small towns where they still attracted crowds. By 1964 the team was no more, but their history is on view at the Negro League's Baseball Museum at 1601 E. 18th.

In 1955, Arnold Johnson, a Chicago businessman who owned New York's Yankee Stadium, brought the major league Philadelphia Athletics to Kansas City. The grandstand roof of the old stadium, now called Municipal Stadium, was jacked up in order to put a second deck under it to enlarge the seating capacity to 32,000. Former President Harry S. Truman threw out the first ball of the 1955 season and attendance at the games hit over a million that year. Kansas City's fans loved the A's.

It can't be said that Kansas City loved the next owner of the team. When Arnold Johnson died unexpectedly in the spring of 1960, his family sold the team to Charles O. Finley, a wealthy Chicago insurance company owner. During the seven years that Finley was in town, the team was in constant chaos. He fired 12 managers and kept threatening to pull the A's out of Kansas City. The American League got Finley to sign a four-year agreement to keep the team in Kansas City. When that expired in 1967, he moved the Athletics to Oakland, California. After having a baseball team for over 80 years, Kansas City was now without one.

A commitment came from the American League that Kansas City could have an expansion club in 1969. Ewing Kauffman agreed to put up the money needed to acquire the team and then underwrite it until it could sustain itself. He paid $10 million for the franchise and put together an organization that would give Kansas City a World Series winner.

"Mr. K" was a self-made man who had lived in Kansas City since he was eight years old. He graduated from Westport High School and then served in the Navy during the Second World War. Afterward, he went to work as a salesman for a pharmaceutical company, making many friends among physicians and druggists in the Midwest. He read every medical journal he could find to become aware of the trends in the pharmaceutical industry.

In 1950 Kauffman started Marion Laboratories out of his basement. He bought vitamins from manufacturers and packaged them under his company's label. He took to the road to sell Marion's products to those physicians and druggists he had developed friendships with.

Ewing Kauffman was a great salesman and knew how to inspire those he hired to become great salesmen. The volume of sales of Marion Labs' products soon needed more salesmen and larger office space. Working hard and deftly expanding his product line made a success of the company. As the business grew, he instigated a profit-sharing plan that he later said made at least 300 of his employees millionaires. By 1965, Marion shares were publicly traded on the stock market.

Kauffman used his organizational skills and salesmanship to help guide the Royals to success. The team started out playing in the old Municipal Stadium. In 1973, the team celebrated moving into the new ballpark at Truman Sports Complex by hosting the major league's all-star game. The Royals were in the 1980 World Series but lost, and they were in the 1981 and 1984 playoffs but didn't win. However, Kansas City fans supported their team with near-capacity crowds at home games.

In 1983, Kauffman sold half of his interest in the Royals to Avron Fogelman, a developer from Memphis, Tennessee. It was Kauffman's plan to eventually sell the remainder to Fogelman, too. However, by 1990 the developer's investments had suffered severe losses and Kauffman was forced to buy back Fogelman's share of the team.

When the Royals won the 1985 "I-70" or "Show Me" World Series playing against the St. Louis Cardinals, Kansas City fans went wild. Businesses and schools closed so everyone could attend the team's welcoming home parade. Cheering fans lined up hours before the parade started, several people deep along the parade route from downtown to the Liberty Memorial. Thousands of pounds of confetti and shredded paper were thrown during the parade. It was a celebration that Kansas City fans would not forget.

Mr. Kauffman had not been able to find a partner who would invest in the Royals and eventually buy him out. In the spring of 1993 he presented a plan that would keep the Royals in Kansas City for at least six years after his death. The plan proposed that local philanthropists contribute $50 million to be banked toward the team's future, and the interest would be used to pay the Royals' operating expenses. At Kauffman's death, the team would be managed by a group of civic leaders. When the team was sold, the money from the sale would go to the Greater Kansas City Community Foundation. Those who had contributed to the plan could then donate their share to any charitable organization they wished. Kauffman's estate would donate sufficient money to pay the Royals' projected yearly losses during the transition time. At the time the plan was announced, Mr. and Mrs. Kauffman pledged $10 million toward the $50 million needed.

Ewing Kauffman died August 1, 1993. His wife and partner in the Royals, Muriel Kauffman, died March 17, 1995. In May 1995, the Internal Revenue Service approved the Kauffmans' plan to keep the Royals in Kansas City. The major-league owners gave their approval. The rest of the $50 million was raised and in June, 1995, the Greater Kansas City Community Foundation became the owners of the Royals. According to the Kauffman's wishes, if there isn't a local buyer within six years, the Royals can be sold to another city.

Early football in Kansas City centered around the competition between the University of Missouri and the University of Kansas teams. Their first game took place on October 31, 1890, at Exposition Park on 15th Street. Three thousand people paid 50 cents apiece to see the game, which Kansas won. The MU-KU games were played in Kansas City in various parks every Thanksgiving Day. The colleges' alumni would arrive days ahead by special trains from all over the country. The Coates House Hotel at 10th and Broadway was the Kansas headquarters, and the Midland Hotel at 7th and Walnut was where Missouri fans stayed. The two student bands paraded back and forth in the streets between the two hotels, playing their school songs. In 1911 the playoff game was moved to the campuses, alternating between them each year.

In 1924 Kansas City had a professional football team in the NFL called the Cowboys, made up of players from the Midwest colleges. However, the team got little local support and lasted only three years.

Thirty-six years passed before Kansas City had another professional football team. In 1962, wealthy Texan Lamar Hunt proposed bringing the Dallas Texans, champions of 1962 American Football League, to Kansas City. In five weeks the Chamber of Commerce sold more advance tickets, totalling $600,000, than 13 of the 22 franchises. The advance sales and Mayor H. Roe Bartle's offer to lease Municipal Stadium at a dollar a year for the first two years was enough to convince Hunt. The team played their first season here in 1963.

The Kansas City Star ran a contest to name the new football team and over a thousand entries came in from 21 states. It was decided to call them the Chiefs in honor of Mayor Bartle, as this had been his nickname since his days of running the local Boy Scout organization. The fans were enthusiastic even though the Chiefs didn't win many games during their first three seasons in Kansas City. But the team got better, and in 1967 they made it to the first Super Bowl (they lost, however, to the Green Bay Packers).

The team got another chance. In the 1970 Super Bowl the Kansas City Chiefs defeated the Minnesota Vikings 23 to 7, and an estimated 250,000 fans welcomed the winners home. They made the playoff game again in 1971, but, in the longest game in football history, they lost to the Miami Dolphins. Even though the Chiefs have made several playoffs, they have yet to play in another Super Bowl.

The city's basketball history is intertwined with the history of the Kansas City Athletic Club, started in 1893 in a hall at Ninth and Central next to a horse stable. The club had a handball court, some gymnasium equipment, and one goal for the new game called "basketball." In 1899 the club was incorporated to "provide a club house and gymnasium for the lawful amusement of its members and for the encouragement and promotion of athletic and field sports."

In 1905 KCAC's basketball team made sports headlines when they beat the Buffalo Germans. In a three-game series played on Convention Hall's concrete floor, they beat the Germans, who had won the Pan-American Games at the St. Louis World's Fair. In those days, players didn't wear any protective elbow and knee pads, and after the games they all had plenty of scrapes and bruises.

After the big win, KCAC's membership more than doubled to 1,000. The club built a three-story building at 1016 Central with a swimming pool and a large gym. KCAC also purchased land on Gillham Road south of Linwood Boulevard, where they had baseball diamonds, tennis courts, a running track, and a swimming pool.

The club's membership kept expanding. Soldiers returning from the First World War joined, and when KCAC's basketball team won the Amateur Athletic Union national basketball championship in 1921 before a crowd of 6,000 at Convention Hall, the membership jumped to 2,000.

Because their facilities on Central couldn't hold all of their members, the club launched a fund-raising campaign to buy a 22-story unfinished building on the northwest corner of 11th and Baltimore. The new club, which opened in 1923, included handball courts, a boxing ring, a running track, 300 guest rooms, a ballroom, a roof garden, and a swimming pool.

The hard times during the Depression reduced the membership numbers, and by 1933 there were only 220 members. The building was converted into the Continental Hotel, but the club retained four floors. In the late 1980s the hotel was renovated into an office building. After almost a century in operation, KCAC went out of existence, but the marble inlaid swimming pool remains.

F. C. "Phog" Allen, basketball coach at the University of Kansas for 39 years, was responsible for getting the National Collegiate Athletic Association's Western playoffs and championship games to Kansas City's Municipal Auditorium in 1940. Because KU and MU games had created a large number of basketball fans in Kansas City, the games were guaranteed big crowds. Almost 16,000 were there for the 1940 NCAA tournament to see the KU Jayhawks win over Southern California. The title games stayed in Kansas City for three years and then moved to Madison Square Garden.

In April 1988, when the NCAA's Final Four was played at the Kemper Arena, 20,000 fans were there to see KU win over Oklahoma. As of the 1994-95 season the Final Four is played in a different city each year. The Big Eight Conference tournament soon to be the Big Twelve, is still played in Kansas City. NCAA's Visitors Center is located in Overland Park, Kansas, and is open to the public.

In 1949 there was an attempt to organize a professional basketball team in Kansas City. The HiSpots, in the U.S. Basketball League, lasted less than one season. And the Kansas City Steers played in the American Basketball League playoffs in 1962. The league only lasted a year and a half, and so did the Steers. In 1972 the Cincinnati Royals moved here. Later the team was renamed the Kings. At first it was a shared franchise, known as the Kansas City-Omaha Kings.

The Kings peaked in the 1978-79 season, attracting over 10,000 to their games. By the early 1980s, however, ticket sales had dropped, and in 1985 the team moved to Sacramento, California. Kansas City then got a Continental basketball franchise and the Sizzlers came to town. They lasted only one year. At present there is no professional basketball team playing in the city.

In 1986 the University of Missouri–Kansas City started to build a basketball team with an eye toward getting into the NCAA Big Eight. Their team, the Kangaroos, played in the Municipal Auditorium Arena, the Kemper Arena and the new Swinney Recreation Center on UMKC's campus. By 1993 they were drawing an average of 3,000 loyal fans per game.

Horse racing began in Kansas City with the harness races in the 1874 agricultural fair. From 1883 to 1886, horses raced in Westport. A track and a three-deck grandstand was situated near 36th Street from Jefferson east to Broadway. Racing fans came from all over the Midwest by special trains to Union Depot and took a horse-drawn streetcar to

Westport. In 1904 the Elm Ridge racecourse stretched between 59th and 63rd east of The Paseo. There were stables for 800 horses, and a clubhouse was built at 63rd and Virginia. For 19 days in April 1904, the first Kansas City Derby was run at Elm Ridge. Seventy-five thousand dollars in prizes was given away. After the law against pari-mutuel betting was enforced, Elm Ridge closed. The land was later used for the Blue Hills Golf Club.

In 1927 Kansas City's political boss Tom Pendergast and an associate bought the old Fairview greyhound racetrack in Riverside, Missouri and turned it into a horse track. Although officially called "Riverside Park Jockey Club," some called it "Riverside Downs" and many others referred to it as "Pendergast's Track." The track had 15 stables with stalls for 800 horses, rooms for 60 jockeys, and a 12,000 seat capacity grandstand that was filled most days of the racing season.

Horse owners from around the country, including many famous movie stars, brought their horses to race at Riverside. Pendergast, an owner himself, became addicted to gambling on horse races. He poured over *The Racing Form* and, using long distance telephone and telegraph, placed bets at tracks all over the country. The Riverside track stayed open until 1937. The grandstand stood where the Red X grocery store is today.

Kansas Citians had two Kentucky Derby winners. In 1890 Ed-

The Riverside Park's grandstand had special ticket windows for women bettors.

ward Corrigan's Riley won the Derby. Herbert Woolf, owner of Kansas City's Woolf Brothers stores, had the winning entry in the 1938 Kentucky Derby. His horse, Lawrin, was ridden to victory by a new jockey named Eddie Arcaro.

Early auto racing was also held at Elm Ridge. Barney Oldfield, the first man to drive a car at a speed of a mile a minute, raced there in 1907. In the 1920s there was an auto racetrack east of 95th and Troost where today Allied Signal and the large federal complex is located. There was an auto racetrack in Riverside and midget auto races run at the Olympic track at 15th Street near the Blue River.

Golf got started in Kansas City at the Hyde Park Country Club, an exclusive organization for the residents of the Hyde Park neighborhood. The golf course was located near today's 37th and Gillham Road. Friends of the residents wanted to golf, too, and the links became crowded. It was decided to relocate the club to the east pasture of the Seth Ward farm, west of Wornall Road and south of 51st Street. In 1896 the nine-hole Kansas City Country Club golf course opened on 111 acres. This was historic ground. For awhile, when golfers sliced too deep, they came up with more than divots: bullets left over from the Battle of Westport came up with the grass. For a time there was a polo club and stables on the course. But golf players complained about the stench and the flies, and the polo club moved east across Wornall Road. In 1926 the Ward family refused to renew the club's lease. The organization moved across State Line to 62nd and Indian Lane. In 1927 Mrs. Jacob Loose purchased 75 acres of the former golf course and gave it to the city for a park as a memorial to her husband.

Bicycle clubs were all the rage just before and after the turn of the 20th century. In the 1880s bicycles had high wheels and were not easy to mount or to ride. Further, since these early bikes had no brakes, maneuvering them could be precarious. The riders were mostly men.

The first bicycle club was organized in 1882, and the members held races on the old racetrack in Westport. "The Outing Cyclists" took their bicycles with them on a train to Leavenworth and pedaled around the fort. The club members also took the interurban train to Olathe and rode on the dirt roads, often stopping at farmhouses to eat strawberries and cream.

The Kansas City Cyclists Club was organized in 1898 when the "low" or safety bicycle and gas balloon tires became popular. Women and youngsters joined the bike riders (some of the bolder ladies wore bloomers). Many of the clubs took long rides on weekends, the favorites being to Lee's Summit and Independence. Some clubs would take the ferry across the Missouri River and ride to Parkville or to Liberty. Once a year the Kansas City Cyclists Club rode to Eastern Jackson County to eat corn on the cob at a farm.

When cars became affordable, the bicycle clubs declined. However, bike riding has never gone out of style. People still ride for pleasure and exercise, and acquiring a bike is still a rite of passage for many Kansas City kids.

Riding a bicycle was a group sport in the 1880s and '90s. Bicycle clubs were where the guys hung out together.

ENTERTAINING KANSAS CITY

Scarcely had the forest been cleared around the early settlers' cabins when they started having dances. Joe and Peter Rivard, who came with the Chouteaus from St. Louis, played their fiddles and everyone danced. Madame Chouteau ordered a piano from St. Louis to add to the music. Father Bernard Donnelley recorded in his journal that musical evenings at the Chouteaus included sing-a-longs of "Yankee Doodle" and "Turkey in the Straw."

A circus boat stopped at the levee for the first time in 1846 and brought the first elephant to town. Circuses traveled on special steamboats, and their animals, clowns, and acrobats performed right on deck. Circuses continued to arrive every year, sometimes several times a year. Their bands, clowns, and brightly painted wagons paraded the streets to attract audiences. They performed in the Public Square. P.T. Barnum's three-ring circus started coming to Kansas City by train in 1881, pitching tents at 15th and Chestnut. Later there were circus grounds at 17th and Indiana and in the 1930s and '40s near Belmont and St. John. Later, they were moved to North Kansas City, and then the circuses moved indoors to the Municipal Auditorium.

Performers traveling to gold-rich California stepped off their steamboats here, preparing to go overland the rest of the way. While in the town they picked up some money doing their acts. In the mid-l850s, concerts and melodramas were given in churches, in the courthouse, and at the public square.

The early so-called theaters were really just big rooms above stores or saloons. Lockridge Hall, said to be Kansas City's first theater, was on the second floor of a building erected in 1858 over a public sewer on Main Street between Fifth and Sixth. Two years later the underground sewer settled, causing Lockridge Hall to drop several feet into a big hole. Audiences in these theaters were men; women, certainly respectable women, didn't attend. By 1866 the audiences had gotten so rambunctious that soldiers were stationed at some theaters to prevent brawling.

Performances of every kind were staged at Long's Hall, above a bakery and saloon (a ready concession stand). Frank's Hall, on the northwest corner of Fifth and Main, also a second-floor theater, was where the diminutive Tom Thumb, star of P.T. Barnum's circus, made an appearance in 1864. The crowd was such that, because he was only 40 inches tall and weighed only 70 pounds, Mr. Thumb had to be carried through the mob. The throng pushed closer and wouldn't make way. The next day the newspaper reported, "Mr. Thumb turned on the volume and using profanity cleared a pathway to the stage."

In 1869 a performance of the "can-can" at Frank's Hall was too risque for the town—a city law said that a female's limbs must be covered to below the knees. The producer was fined $16. (In 1916 the famous Paris Ballet Russe was in town to give a performance at Convention Hall. Kansas City's police chief thought people dancing in tights was immoral and told their manager, Sergei Diaghilev, "This is strictly a moral town and we won't stand for any of that highbrow immorality." However, the performance was allowed to go on and the review in *The Kansas City Star* said "Ballet won Kansas City.")

Kersey Coates built Kansas City's first real theater. The Coates Opera House, costing $100,000, opened in 1871 on the northwest corner of 10th and Broadway. It stood just across from the Coates House Hotel, said to be the finest between St. Louis and California.

The Coates Opera House was the center of the town's cultural life for over 30 years and made theater going respectable for women. Every important actor, singer, and musician in the country performed on the Coates stage. On January 31, 1901, just a half hour after closing, a fire broke out and the theater burned to the ground, never to be rebuilt.

The success of the Coates Opera House prompted the building of the Gillis Opera House in 1883 on Fifth Street from Walnut to Main. It was here that the famous French actress Sarah Bernhardt first appeared in Kansas City. (She demanded to be paid in gold before she would perform and kept the gold in a coffin.) The Gillis, too, would meet a fiery end. On June 25, 1925, an explosion at 11 p.m. demolished the Gillis Theater and almost the entire block. Fifty persons died and 30 were injured. The theater's chorus line had just finished performing, and many of the girls were next door at Sanderson's Lunch eating an evening snack. They were buried in debris when the restaurant's ceiling and walls collapsed from the blast. The fire burned all night because firemen couldn't contain the flames. It was later discovered that dynamite being used a few blocks away to level Hobo Hill (the former Pearl Street) had caused the earth to move under the theater and rupture the antiquated gas pipes, which then exploded. A new, smaller Gillis Theater rose on the site. That building is still there but much altered. The theater's name is above the southwest doorway.

Theater building flourished in the 1880s and '90s. They were located near the Market Square, sometimes several to a block. Some presented melodramas, but most theaters offered variety shows—a mixture of song, dance, and comedy that later evolved into vaudeville. The Free and Easy Theater at Fourth and Main was appropriately named. It featured situations and dialogue that were vulgar and sometimes obscene. The Theater Comique at Fourth and Walnut offered shows that were the forerunner of burlesque. The Comique served beer and was next to the Jackson County Horse Railroad stables.

As the town moved south, so did theaters. Before electricity gas lamps were used to light the stage. Fire was always a hazard. The theaters were required to have an asbestos curtain that could be lowered to protect the audience in case flames broke out backstage. Fire destroyed

The second Orpheum Theater just south of 12th Street on Baltimore.

the Ninth Strcet Theatre built at Ninth and May Street in 1891. The Orpheum Theatre was erected on the site. A part of the Keith Orpheum circuit, the theater booked touring vaudeville acts, changing every week and offering family fare. Tickets cost 25 cents for the balcony and 50 cents downstairs.

In 1914 a more ornate Orpheum was built on the west side of Baltimore between 12th and 13th to attract the visitors staying at the Muehlebach and Baltimore Hotels. This theater offered more sophisticated touring plays. By the 1940s it was primarily a movie house, occasionally offering plays. In 1961 the Orpheum was torn down to make way for the construction of the Hotel Muehlebach's ballroom.

The Warder Grand Theater, at Ninth and Holmes, was not finished when it opened October 26, 1887. There was no roof, no heat, and chairs had to be borrowed from a funeral parlor. The opening production was *Othello* starring Edwin Booth, brother of Abraham Lincoln's assassin. The audience watched the performance huddled in blankets. The next day *The Kansas City Times* said, "Mr. Booth succeeded in rousing a good deal of enthusiasm, not withstanding the adverse conditions."

At the turn of the 20th century there were theaters presenting live performances all over downtown Kansas City. But as silent films became popular, their audiences dwindled. Some of these theaters held on into the early 1930s. Only three of these buildings remain today. The Grand Opera House, on the southwest corner of Seventh and Walnut (where Harry Truman used to usher so he could see the show free) is today a garage. The Mainstreet at 14th and Main, built in 1921 to present vaudeville, is boarded up. Butler's Standard Theater built in 1900 at 12th and Central became The Standard, then The Century, and in 1941 The Folly (because it presented burlesque). Restored in 1981, many performing organizations use the Folly Theater today.

The first demonstration of silent films was shown at the Coates Opera House in 1897. Three short films were shown, including the controversial *The Kiss*, which showed a couple embrace and kiss and thus shocked thc audience. The year before, Kansas Citian George Curtis obtained a motion picture camera and filmed downtown street scenes, including cable cars at the Junction. The Kansas City Museum has a copy of this film. A silent feature called *Two Girls and One Bonnet* was made here in 1916 by the Missouri Historical Association. Their members were the actors in the film, but it was not a success.

By 1910 there were over 100 movie theaters in Kansas City—

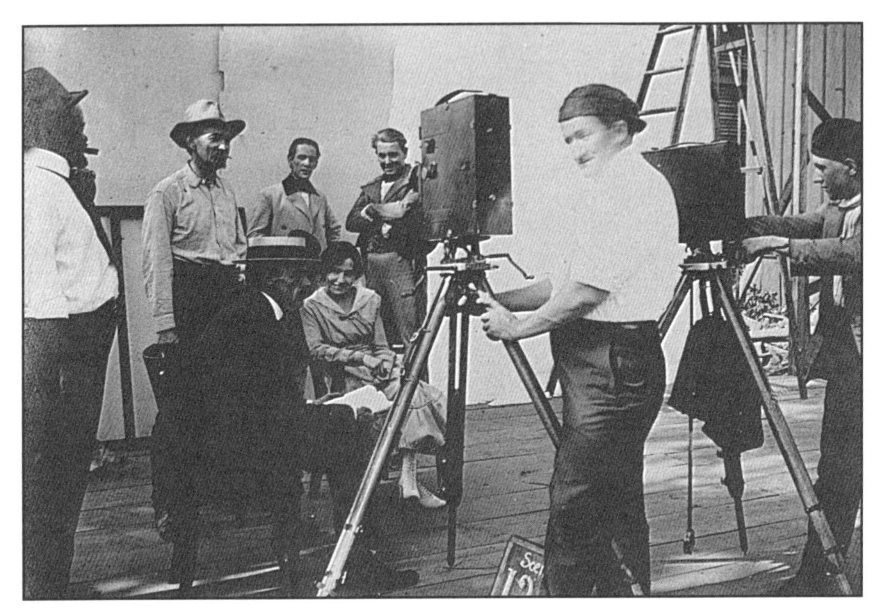

The silent film "Two Girls and One Bonnet," was made in Kansas City in 1916. The camerman was also the director.

several in every neighborhood and Downtown several to each block. They were designed and decorated to look like palaces.

The Globe Theater, built in 1913 on the southwest corner of 13th and Walnut, was where *The Jazz Singer*, the first "talkie," played in 1927. Crowds waiting to hear Al Jolson sing in the movie lined up several blocks to buy tickets. Sound films made moviegoing more popular than ever. The Depression didn't stop people from attending these movie theaters, but television did.

Neighborhood theaters started closing in the mid-1950s when Kansas Citians began staying home to watch TV. Some downtown theaters struggled to stay open into the 1960s. All but one eventually were destroyed to make way for parking lots and office buildings. The Midland Theater, built in 1927 at 13th and Main, has been renovated, and today touring Broadway shows often perform there.

Perhaps one of the most successful and influential movie producers in Hollywood spent some of his boyhood here and started filming cartoons in Kansas City. Walt Disney came to Kansas City with his family from Marceline, Missouri, in 1911, when he wasn't quite 10 years old. His father bought a *Kansas City Star* paper route, and Walt and his brother Roy got up every morning at 3:30 to throw papers to 2,000 customers before they went to school.

Walt wasn't the best of students at Benton School, sometimes falling asleep at his desk because he got up so early. In the fifth grade, he made a high cardboard hat and paper beard, put on his father's frock coat, and appeared before his class as Abe Lincoln and gave the Gettysburg Address. The attention Walt received from his classmates and teachers sparked his interested in performing. It was also at Benton School that he began drawing cartoons.

The summer after he graduated from grade school, his parents and sister moved to Chicago. Walt and Roy stayed in Kansas City, living in the family's home on Bellefontaine. Walt got a job selling peanuts, popcorn, and newspapers aboard trains leaving Union Station. In the fall of 1917 he joined the family in Chicago and went on to high school, where he drew cartoons for the school's paper. Three nights a week he attended the Chicago Institute of Art.

Roy enlisted in the Navy during World War I. Walt, even though only 16, also tried to enlist, but he was too young. Because the Red Cross Ambulance Corps would take him at 17, he lied about his age and joined. A case of the Spanish influenza stopped him from going to France until the war was over. (The flu killed more Americans than the war did.) The day before turning 17, Walt landed in France, where he drove ambulances and handed out coffee and doughnuts at soldiers' canteens.

Walt returned to Kansas City in 1919 and moved into the Bellefontaine house with his two brothers. A series of jobs as an artist taught him about film cartooning and animation. He set up an art studio in the garage behind his house and started his own freelance business with his friend, Ubbe Iwerks, making short cartoons that he hoped to sell to movie theaters. (It was said that Ubbe, who later went to work for Disney in California, was a better artist than Walt and came up with the familiar figure of Mickey Mouse.)

In 1922 the partners moved into the second-floor space of an office building at 1127 E. 31st. They made a sample of "Laugh-O-Grams" cartoons and sold a series to the Newman Theatre at 11th and Main. Walt assembled his staff by advertising that he would give free animation lessons to budding artists in exchange for their working for him. He soon had a staff. However, he sold his Laugh-O-Grams so cheaply there was no profit.

Walt got a New York film distributor interested in a cartoon of *Alice in Wonderland* using animation and a live actress playing Alice. He was able to raise some money from local investors and worked his staff around the clock to make the deadline. Most of the staff quit because they hadn't received any pay, and Walt couldn't complete the project.

Discouraged and owing thousands of dollars, Walt sold his movie camera and went to Los Angeles where his brother Roy was living. After several disappointing tries at creating cartoons for various distributors, Walt came up with an idea that worked. In 1928 Mickey Mouse debuted in *Steamboat Willie*, the first synchronized sound cartoon. Walt supplied Mickey's voice. The mouse became one of the biggest stars in Hollywood and made Disney an instant success.

The first amusement park in Kansas City was Tivoli Gardens, built in 1878 where Crown Center is today. German immigrants lived in the area and frequented the brewery in the park. There was also a dance pavilion and gardens.

Most of the city's early parks were built to get people to ride the new street railways. After the Kansas City Cable Car Company extended their line out Troost in 1888, the company built an amusement park at 27th and Troost. The park was known for its thrilling "Shoot-The-Chute" ride that swung people out over the Troost Lake. Shakespeare's plays also were presented there.

Willard Winner was president of the Independence and Park Railway. (Because the steam engine was covered with canvas to keep from frightening cows and horses as it traveled through farmland, the train was called "The Dummy Line.") To get people to ride his railroad, in 1887 Winner built Mount Washington Amusement Park, between 15th Street and Winner Road. Today a cemetery has replaced the park.

Forest Park was located in 1903 at the end of the Independence Avenue cable car line on the south side of Independence Avenue at Hardesty. It had an English carousel and a monkey house.

To get people to use his interurban "Air Line" from Kansas City to Independence, Arthur Stillwell built Fairmount Park just off 24 Highway. There were rides and a lake for boating and swimming.

The grandest of Kansas City's amusement parks were the two Electric Parks. The first was built because of a streetcar line from the Market Square to the Heims brewery on Montgall in the East Bottoms. (The Heims brothers were the biggest beer suppliers in town.) Joe, Mike, and Fred Heims had built the streetcar line at a cost of $96,000, hoping to get thirsty customers to come to the brewery and buy fresh beer. But it didn't work. In 1899 the brothers built an amusement park at Chestnut and Guinotte near their brewery to attract streetcar riders. Because electricity was new to Kansas City, they called it Electric Park and lit the facility at night, attracting people who worked during the day. The park was such a success that the Heims later sold their streetcar line for $250,000.

Electric Park had rides, fountains, gardens, a vaudeville theater, a dance pavilion, and an immense beer garden modeled after those in Europe. To keep the beer flowing, there was a direct pipeline from the brewery to the beer garden. And because dancing was the only way couples were permitted to hold each other in public, the pavilion was very popular. Special trains brought people to the park from all over the Midwest. Indians, from their reservations in the Kansas Territory, came to ride the roller coaster.

As the city limits expanded to the south, the Heims brothers felt that Electric Park had to move south, too. They dismantled their park and moved to 47th and The Paseo. The second Electric Park was much larger than the other and offered more to do and see. It had a roller coaster, a carousel, a scenic railway, a "dip" coaster, a skating rink, an alligator farm, two dance pavilions, theaters, a dime museum, a bowling alley, a swimming pool, a penny arcade, a shooting gallery, and more. Every night at dusk, with much musical fanfare, young women dressed in near-transparent chiffon and bathed in light emerged from the colorful main fountains. It was a big attraction.

One hundred thousand electric lights made the 27-acre Electric Park glow in the dark.

A fire in 1925 destroyed most of the park's buildings. The dance pavilion was repaired and dances continued. The swimming pool was open until 1934, when another fire occurred. That was the end of Electric Park. The rusted rails of the roller coaster reminded people of the park that once had been. They were finally taken down in the 1950s to make way for the Village Green Apartments built on the site.

Fairyland Park was constructed at 75th and Prospect in 1923. It had many rides, including the Sky Rocket roller coaster, a large swimming pool, and a dance pavilion. In the '20s, '30s, and '40s, couples came to Fairyland to win trophies in dance contests. Besides employing local musicians, big name bands played there, including the Glenn Miller and the Count Basie bands.

Fairyland's Sky Rocket seemed to attract lightning. In 1938 and 1941 the park was severely damaged by lightning strikes. The dance pavilion caught fire in 1943, and 10,000 people had to evacuate the park. When Worlds of Fun opened north of the river in 1973, people went there instead of Fairyland. The park closed in 1977.

The early amusement parks made dancing popular. And there was no more popular place to take a partner than the Pla-Mor, opened in November 1927 at 32nd and Main. The ballroom could hold more than 500 couples and the dance floor was always crowded. It was built on more than 7,000 felt spring cushions, giving dancers a lighter-than-air feeling. Nationally known big bands played here, too.

There were other activities at Pla-Mor. There was a bowling alley and an ice skating rink where the Ice Capades appeared almost every year. During the 1940s, dance marathons were held in the ballroom where contestants danced for weeks, sleeping in each other's arms to be the last couple standing in order to win the grand prize. The Pla-Mor closed in 1951 and the building was demolished in 1972.

Kansas City had military bands quite early, and the town loved parades. Every occasion that residents thought warranted a parade would bring out bands, men in uniform (marching or on horseback), flags and banners, and cheering crowds.

The Priests of Pallas celebration began in 1887 as a parade to attract customers to businesses around the City Market area. It was such a success that it grew into a city-wide, week-long celebration that many said rivaled the New Orleans Mardi Gras. This annual fall event lasted for over 35 years. It started when the Flambeau Club, a group of young businessmen, organized the first Priests of Pallas. They wanted the pa-

Businesses and individuals entered floats in the Priests of Pallas parades. Some of them showed remarkable creativity.

rade to have an air of mystery, so it was named for the Greek goddess of science, the arts, and wisdom.

The first celebration, held during the second week of October 1887, had an added attraction. President Grover Cleveland, in town to lay the cornerstone for the YMCA building at 10th and Oak, watched the third-night parade from a viewing stand.

Thousands took part in the parades, and they drew tens of thousands of spectators from all over the area. The first night was the civic and military procession, which included the Kansas City Light Cavalry, six companies of the Third Regiment, and military bands from many cities close by. Torch bearers walked along the route to light the way. The Flambeau Club, 150 strong, marched in their long white coats. Each member carried a big bag of Roman candles, which they lit along the way, showering the spectators with colorful sparks and swirls of smoke.

The second night's parade was for the trade associations in town. These laborers wanted to outdo the gentry. The union members marched in their best suits, and their bands appeared in bright uniforms. Participants had elaborate floats that were mounted on flat wagons and pulled by beautiful horses. This parade was just as grand as the one the night before.

Queen Athena led the last night of the parades. The theme of the celebration, Grecian mythology, was carried out in over 20 floats. The queen's float had an honor guard of 200 masked businessmen dressed as French cavaliers (how this fit into the Grecian theme wasn't explained). Athena's gown was the palest of pink chiffon over white satin, trimmed in ermine and pearl—and worn by a man in a wig. That night there was a gala ball by invitation only. All important, or near important, people in town coveted the invitations. For many, this was the social event of the year.

The celebration was such a success that it returned year after year, each time trying to outdo the previous event. The themes ranged from mythology to fairytales. Soon there was a whole week of parades, including a daytime children's procession. Residents and visitors looked forward to the yearly celebration. Priests of Pallas was a week devoted to parades, spectacles, dances, and merrymaking. By 1913, however, the town decided it was too sophisticated for such frivolity, and the celebration was canceled. The parade was revived in 1922, when for the first time a woman portrayed Athena, but by 1924 it was gone again and Athena no longer reigned over Kansas City.

Two bands, playing completely different styles of music, came out of Kansas City in the 1920s and became famous all over the world. The Coon-Sanders Nighthawks band owed its success to WDAF radio. The station, owned by *The Kansas City Star,* was the city's first. As soon as it went on the air in 1922, WDAF started broadcasting "The Merry Old Chief" show every midnight. The Chief, former *Star* reporter Leo J. Fitzpatrick, was very much like today's latenight TV hosts. He told stories, exchanged gossip, and recited poetry.

Broadcast lines were soon hooked up between the station and the Hotel Muehlebach to pick up the popular Coon-Sanders orchestra's midnight performance at the hotel. Because there was little on the airways at that time of night and WDAF's signal was powerful, the band was not

The first band to be carried live over a radio station—Kansas City's WDAF—was the Coon-Sanders band.

only heard from coast to coast but had listeners in Canada, the British Isles, and even Australia and Hawaii. The radios were crystal sets then, and people listening through headphones stayed up late to find interesting shows on the radio dial.

One night while they were on the air, one of the musicians said, "If you're up this late to hear us, you must be a nighthawk." The station started receiving letters and telegrams from people all over, saying that they were nighthawks. The band took the name, becoming "The Coon-Sanders Nighthawks." A fan club was organized, and by the next year over 37,000 nighthawks had joined.

Carleton Coon grew up in Sedalia, Missouri, and met Joe Sanders when he came to Kansas City in 1918. Sanders, from Archie, Missouri, was playing the piano at the Jenkins Music Store downtown, demonstrating new tunes to would-be buyers of sheet music. The next year the two formed a small band to perform at local clubs. They became the house band at the Newman Theater at 12th and Main. By 1922 the band was playing at noon at the Hotel Baltimore and at midnight at the Muehlebach Hotel. Their music was described as "razzmatazz."

Because of the radio exposure and the response of their fans, the Nighthawks were in demand outside of Kansas City, too. The group started playing one-night stands around the Midwest in 1923. By 1925 they were appearing at Chicago's Hotel Congress and packing them in. They moved to Chicago's Blackhawk Restaurant and were carried live on a weekly radio show over station WGN. It was said that Al Capone was a fan and made requests for his favorite tunes.

The band went on to perform in New York and made records. They were at the height of their popularity when Carleton Coon died unexpectedly in 1932. Joe Sanders tried to hold the band together, but the group fell apart. He organized another orchestra and continued to perform, but never attained the kind of popularity that the Nighthawks had. Sanders returned to Kansas City and died in obscurity in 1965.

Kansas City style jazz grew out of ragtime and blues. In 1923 the Billy King Road Show was organized here. While playing in Oklahoma City in 1925, the band was reorganized as Walter Page's Original Blue Devils. Out of this band came Count Basie and many who would join Bennie Moten's band. The Devils were called a "territorial band" because they toured throughout the Midwest and Southwest.

Bennie Moten was born in Kansas City in 1894 and started playing ragtime piano in his teens. Moten brought jazz to Kansas City in 1921

Bennie Moten (standing to the left of the piano) and his band in 1926. (Goin' to Kansas City Collection, courtesy of The Kansas City Museum.)

when he organized the BB&D band. The group was soon playing at the Panama Club near 18th and Vine. The sound attracted a record contract, and Moten made his first recording in 1923. The band got so popular that Moten organized a second one to cover engagements in Kansas City while his group was playing out of town.

The Moten band and the Blue Devils often met in Kansas City in a battle of the bands. The musicians would play into the early morning hours until they stopped from exhaustion. The audience would declare the winner and usually the Blue Devils won.

William Basie was born in Red Bank, New Jersey, in 1904. He said that he received his first jazz lesson from Fats Waller, who was performing in a club in Harlem. Basie recounted that Waller saw him moving his hands to try to imitate Waller's playing, and the legendary piano man invited Basie to sit beside him and get a lesson in jazz.

In his early 20s, Basie was playing piano accompaniment to the silent movies in theaters. He got a job with a touring vaudeville band that brought him to Kansas City. The troupe went broke here and Basie was stranded. He found a job playing piano for the movies at the Eblon Theater on Vine. At one of the clubs on 18th Street, he met Walter Page, who invited him to join the Blue Devils. When the Blue Devils broke up, Basie joined the Moten band in 1929; later, in 1931, Walter Page joined, too.

Eighteenth and Vine was not only the heart of the black community, it was the heart of Kansas City jazz. When the Monarchs baseball team was in town, blacks from all over the Midwest came to see the game and then went to 18th and Vine to visit the jazz clubs.

During this time, political boss Tom Pendergast ruled Kansas City and the town was wide open. Booze, gambling, and prostitution were a part of everyday life. It was said members of the mob—Irish, Italian, Jews and Blacks—ran the clubs or got paid off by other club owners for protection. If Pendergast didn't directly participate, he turned his head and let it happen. But whatever was going on was good for jazz.

More than 200 clubs in Kansas City featured live music. Many of those playing jazz were located along 12th and 18th Streets near the Vine Street intersection. There were other clubs in the city, but this was the highest concentration of jazz. It was said that the clubs never closed. The streets were alive with crowds going in and out of all-night restaurants, gambling joints, and nightclubs.

These clubs' names have become legends in the jazz world: Street's Blue Room, The Hey-Hey Club, The Spinning Wheel, Capitan,

The Cherry Blossom, and The Lone Star. The most famous were the Reno, Sunset, and Subway Clubs. The clubs attracted jazz musicians to Kansas City from all over the country, not only looking for jobs but because of the great musicians here to learn from.

After Basie joined Moten's band, they continued to tour, but the band always came back to Kansas City where they were in demand. They became the house band at the El Torreon Ballroom, where they were broadcast live over KMBC radio three times a week. During the summer the Moten band also was the house band at the Fairyland Park Dance Pavilion, which was open only to white dancers.

In 1935 Bennie Moten went into the hospital to have a simple tonsillectomy and died during the operation. His brother, Buster Moten, took over the band, but it broke apart within a few months. Basie, along with Buster Smith (who had also been with the Blue Devils), gathered the remaining Moten members and started the Buster Smith–Bill Basie Band of Rhythm. The group began playing at the Reno Club, where they were picked up nightly on national short wave radio station W9XBY. The announcer named Basie "Count" and these broadcasts pushed him into "the big time."

In Chicago, John Hammond, who later became a jazz record producer, heard the band on radio. He got Decca Records interested in recording the Basie band and also got the group dates to play Chicago nightclubs. The band left Kansas City in 1936. Within a year Basie's big band was playing clubs in New York and appearing on national radio stations. The Kansas City sound had gone national.

Basie frequently returned to Kansas City for concerts. Seven months before he died in April 1984, Basie was in town. His band, playing in the square at Crown Center, attracted an audience of an estimated 35,000.

Most of the 18th and Vine structures connected with the history of Kansas City jazz are gone. One important building still stands though, just south of 18th Street at 1823 Highland. In 1928 this building became the home of the black musicians' union, Local 627. The union not only looked after the welfare of its members but jam sessions also were held here. It has been said that jam sessions originated in Kansas City and attracted musicians from all over the country. The early sessions were held after hours at clubs, dance halls, theaters, and even pool halls. Today when musicians come to town they can sometimes find a jam going on at the Local 627 building. And when the jazz gets hot, it can last forever.

HEADQUARTERS

Several businesses and institutions that originated in Kansas City during the first half of the 20th century still have their headquarters here. Some businesses, even though they may now be owned by corporations outside of Kansas City, still have factories here. These headquarters have not only added to the city's economy by providing jobs for the local workforce, they have carried Kansas City's name around the world.

In 1902 Kansas Citians Jacob and Joseph Loose and John Wiles started the Loose-Wiles Biscuit Company in the West Bottoms to produce quality bakery products. They felt that natural sunshine was important to their workers, so their plant had many windows. They named their crackers and cookies "Sunshine Biscuits."

Sunshine Biscuits soon became a household name, not only in Kansas City but across the country. The company opened a bakery in Boston and in 1912 built the "Thousand Window Bakery" in Long Island, New York, which until 1955 was the largest bakery in the world.

In 1946 the company's name changed officially to Sunshine Biscuits, Inc. A new Sunshine bakery was built in the Fairfax industrial district in 1949. Its 550-foot continuous oven is the largest in the world. At present, six other Sunshine bakeries operate in the country.

The company was sold to the American Tobacco Company in 1966. Twenty-two years later it was acquired by a privately held corporation, G.G. Industries, Inc., with headquarters in New Jersey. The Fairfax bakery produces the company's Cheez-Its, Krispy Crackers, and Chip-A-Roo cookies. The name of the two founders is still very much a part of Kansas City. Profits from the company's crackers and cookies paid for the land that today is Loose Park.

Four Italian immigrants started a company here in 1913 called the Kansas City Macaroni and Importing Company. By 1917 they were producing their own macaroni in a factory located on Independence Avenue between Campbell and Charlotte, where many women from the nearby Italian community worked. In the early 1920s the company's name changed to The American Beauty Macaroni Company. At that time, pasta was served only in Italian homes and restaurants, and thus American Beauty products were only on the shelves of stores near Italian communities. That changed after the Second World War, when soldiers who had served in Italy came home. Grateful families in Italy had invited American servicemen to share their pasta meals. When the GIs came home they brought their taste for pasta with them. Mainstream grocery stores began carrying American Beauty macaroni. The company soon had factories in Texas, Colorado, Minneapolis, Utah, and California.

The headquarters of America Beauty remained on Independence Avenue until 1957, when the company moved to the Fairfax industrial district. The family of the original founders ran the company until they sold it to the Pillsbury Company in 1977. In 1985 it was purchased by the Hershey Chocolate Company. The American Beauty factory remains in Fairfax.

Hallmark Cards started when 19-year-old Joyce Hall came to Kansas City in 1910 from Norfolk, Nebraska, with a shoebox full of postcards to sell. He took a small room at the YMCA at 10th and Oak and began selling the cards out of the box he kept under his bed.

Hall had become a salesman at the age of nine. When trains stopped at the depot in David City, Nebraska, near the Hall household, he sold the passengers sandwiches he had made at home. He also took a job as a door-to-door salesman representing a women's cosmetics company. When his brothers Rollie and Bill bought a bookstore in Norfolk in 1902, Mrs. Hall, her daughter Marie, and Joyce moved there, too. The 12-year-old Joyce worked at the bookstore while going to school. During the summer Rollie took him along when he traveled to stores in Nebraska, Wyoming, and South Dakota selling candy for an Omaha candy factory.

A turning point in the Halls' lives occurred when a salesman representing a postcard company came into the bookstore trying to get them interested in wholesaling his cards. The brothers invested in the cards and started a business: The Norfolk Post Card Company. Besides selling the cards in the store, Rollie brought them along on his candy-selling route, and during summer vacations from school Joyce sold them to stores throughout Nebraska and South Dakota.

The move to Kansas City, which had better railroad connections and a larger population, was a calculated expansion of their card business. Using maps of Missouri and Kansas, Joyce (he had no middle name until his older brother gave him "Clyde" as one before he left for Kansas City; he later was called "J.C.") sent card samples to small towns, addressed only to The Leading Post Card Dealer. He got orders. Soon the mail order business was going so well that J.C. hired a helper to go on the road selling postcards.

When the YMCA began objecting to the large volume of mail he was receiving, J.C. rented space in a building nearby. He began printing his own postcards with simple messages, and they sold. His mother, sister, and Rollie came to Kansas City, and they all moved into a house on Troost.

In 1913 the brothers added ready-made greeting cards to their sales list. The next year they had 20 engraved Christmas cards produced with "Published by Hall Bros." imprinted on the backs. This was the beginning of Hallmark. The following year, the brothers bought engraving presses and started manufacturing cards themselves.

As the company grew, they moved their offices into several different buildings in downtown Kansas City. Bill Hall joined them in 1920, and by 1923 Hall Bros. was doing well enough to build a six-story factory and office at 26th and Walnut.

Even during the Depression, cards sold well, because people who could not afford to buy gifts could send a 10 or 15-cent greeting instead. In 1936 the Halls acquired a large building at 25th and Grand, which they overhauled for their headquarters. In 1956 Hallmark built its present headquarters at 25th and McGee that connected with this building.

Although the word "Hallmark" first appeared on the backs of cards in 1925, the company didn't officially become Hallmark until 1954. The slogan, "When you care enough to send the very best," was first used in 1944, and the crown trademark was registered in 1949.

Many famous artists have designed cards for Hallmark, including Walt Disney, Norman Rockwell, Grandma Moses, Georgia O'Keeffe, Andrew Wyeth, and even Sir Winston Churchill. The company is the largest employer of artists in the world.

As far back as 1936, Hallmark began buying property surrounding their plants. In 1968 the company started construction on Crown Center, a complex of stores, office buildings, apartments, and hotels west and north of their corporate headquarters. Crown Center opened in 1973, not only revitalizing the central city but changing the look of Kansas City.

Joyce Hall died in 1982. Under the leadership of his son Don, Hallmark Cards and Crown Center continue to bring pride to Kansas City. What began with a teenager from Nebraska and a box of postcards has reached millions around the world.

Shortly after the First World War, a garment business started in Kansas City that continues today as a leader in the industry. Arthur Brookfield, who had taught Greek and Latin at the University of Michigan, moved to Kansas City in 1910. He and a high school friend started a company to make athletic union suits.

After serving in the Quartermaster Corps in World War I, where his job was dealing with textile manufacturers who provided materials for soldiers' uniforms, Brookfield joined a Kansas City clothing manufacturing firm. He developed a mail order division of the company, calling it Unitog Manufacturing. He left the company in 1932, took the mail order business with him, and opened an office at 29th and Main.

Brookfield reasoned that because of the Depression, companies providing service to the public needed to show their stability and reliability. He believed they could do that by dressing their employees in clean and attractive uniforms. He sold the idea to individual gasoline station owners and contracted with a clothing manufacturer to make the uniforms. When Conoco Oil signed a contract with Brookfield to supply uniforms for their service station employees across the country, Unitog opened a factory in Warrensburg, Missouri, just east of Kansas City. Before the Second World War, Unitog was producing coveralls for the Army and uniforms for the Missouri Home Guard. When America entered the war, Unitog got the contract to make fatigues for the Army.

When the war ended, returning GIs bought new cars and moved to the suburbs. Gasoline companies opened many new service stations and created a larger market for attendants' uniforms. Unitog became the primary supplier of uniforms for the service station industry, establishing warehouses on the east and west coast.

Arthur Brookfield died in 1955. His son Dutton, who came into the company in 1939 by working during his summer breaks from the University of Missouri at Columbia, took over. The company kept expanding, providing uniforms for a variety of service industry employees, including the U.S. Postal Service workers.

Dutton Brookfield died in a fire at his Minnesota summer home in 1979, and his son Arthur took over the company. In 1983 a group of Unitog managers bought out the Brookfield family's stock. The company's headquarters remain in downtown Kansas City.

In Denver, Colorado, during 1923, a long-held dream of Mr. and Mrs. Russell Stover got underway. As Clara Stover had long been making hand-dipped chocolate candies in the kitchen of the couple's bungalow home, the pair decided to open their first "Mrs. Stover's Bungalow Candies" store. They thought that giving the shop that name would assure customers that the candy was homemade. The exterior of the store was designed to look like a little house. The Stovers brought their candy company to Kansas City in 1931, and the rest is candy history.

Russell started in the candy business as a salesman for a company in Canada. When he was sent a batch of candy that he found below his standards, he and Clara experimented in their kitchen and substituted their candy for the bad lot. The customers liked it.

The Stovers moved to Des Moines, where Russell managed an ice cream manufacturing company. He bought the company and came up with the Eskimo Pie, a chocolate-covered ice cream treat. It became an immediate sensation across the country and brought high profits that attracted the Wrigley Chewing Gum Company to offer $1.5 million for Stover's company. He turned them down. Soon other ice cream companies began making copycat versions of the Eskimo Pie. Stover tried to fight the imitators in the courts but lost. He sold his company for $30,000 and moved to Denver.

In order to supply their Denver candy store, the Stovers hired seven employees to help Clara in the kitchen. When the store opened, the chocolates sold so well that within two weeks the couple opened another Mrs. Stover's Bungalow Candies. Within a year three more were operating. The Stovers decided to expand to Kansas City and opened two stores and a factory here.

In 1931 the couple moved their headquarters to a building near 12th and Main in downtown Kansas City. By 1939 Mrs. Stover's Candies had 400 employees, six stores in Kansas City, and other stores throughout the Midwest. When Russell Stover died in 1954, the company was producing 11 million pounds of candy a year and had 40 Stover stores. The candy also was sold in 2,000 department stores. Mrs. Stover died in 1975.

The company was operated by the Stovers and their partners for 37 years. In 1969 the enterprise was purchased by Louis Ward and today is an international company. Russell Stover Candies is the largest producer of fine boxed chocolates in the United States. And it all started in Clara's kitchen.

A variety of associations have found Kansas City ideal for their headquarters. The Veterans of Foreign Wars of the United States first moved their headquarters from New York to Kansas City, Kansas, in 1924, occupying a portion of the newly constructed Memorial Building.

A dispute with the building's management in 1930 prompted a move across the state line into a 12-story building at 34th and Broadway in midtown Kansas City, Missouri. In 1946 the VFW bought the building and still uses it as their headquarters.

The Veterans of Foreign Wars evolved out of two organizations founded after the Spanish-American War. Soldiers who had fought in that war were only given $15 on discharge. There were no medical benefits for those who were wounded, nor any money for the families of those who were killed. In 1914 the two groups merged into the Veterans of Foreign Wars of the United States.

As soon as America entered World War I, the VFW successfully lobbied Congress to pass the War Risk Insurance Act to provide medical help for disabled veterans and compensation for the families of those killed in the war. VFW also pushed for veterans to be paid a bonus 20 years after the war. In 1930, during the height of the Depression, 15,000 unemployed veterans marched on Washington, asking for their bonus money to feed their families. President Herbert Hoover denied them their bonuses and called out the Army to drive the former soldiers from the Capital. When Franklin Roosevelt became president, 50 percent of the bonus was paid and fours years later the balance was paid in full in savings bonds.

Today there are over 10,000 VFW posts throughout this country and the world. The VFW represents over 2.1 million veterans from all of the wars fought by Americans in the 20th century.

Farmland Industries got its start in 1929, when six farmer-owned cooperatives joined forces to buy and sell petroleum products under the name of Union Oil Company. Their first offices were in a two-car garage on Iron Street in North Kansas City.

By 1932 the company was selling their products to cooperatives in Missouri, Kansas, Colorado, Nebraska, the Dakotas, Idaho, Washington, and Oregon. The Depression created hard times for farmers, and many saw that by joining cooperatives they could pay less for their supplies and thus help themselves to survive.

Union's name changed to Consumers Cooperation Association in 1934, and the operation moved to a larger, three-story building down the street from the garage. The structure had space for their expanding offices and axle grease plant. By 1936, CCA was selling groceries to their cooperative stores, delivered in trucks with a big "CO-OP" painted on them. In 1938 the co-op built its first refinery, and by the end of the next year CCA was producing more than 200 products and had a membership of 259 cooperatives.

CAA continued to expand, buying feed mills, grain terminals, meat processing plants, fertilizer plants and service stations throughout the region.

In 1944 CCA purchased a five-story building at 10th and Oak in downtown Kansas City for their offices. In 1956 they moved to their world headquarters building on North Oak Trafficway just beyond North Kansas City.

CCA became Farmland Industries, Inc. in 1966. The nation's largest regional agribusiness cooperative, Farmland shows nearly $7 billion in sales annually in 50 states and 85 countries. It is owned by 1,500 farmer-owned cooperatives representing over 1.2 million farmers and ranchers. Farmland is an advocate for its members and offers expertise, technology, and information through the local cooperatives to help farmers and ranchers succeed in the increasingly competitive worldwide agribusiness.

The American Academy of Family Physicians is one of the nation's largest medical organizations, with more than 75,000 members in the 50 states, Washington, D.C., Puerto Rico, the Virgin Islands, and Guam. The Academy started in Kansas City in 1947 under the name of the American Academy of General Practice to promote and maintain high standards for family doctors.

The Academy was instrumental in getting the medical profession to establish family practice as a medical specialty. To bring focus on that specialty, the organization changed its name to the American Academy of Family Physicians in 1971. Its members, who are family doctors, must complete a minimum of 150 hours of approved continuing education every three years. Accurate records are kept to ensure that this requirement is met. The Academy's Annual Scientific Assembly meeting for continuing education draws an average of 17,000 physicians and visitors. The group also publishes *American Family Physician,* a monthly clinical journal for physicians in primary care that has a circulation of 150,000. AAFP headquarters is now located at 88th and Ward Parkway.

Midwest Research Institute got its start in 1943 when civic and industrial leaders from six Midwestern states met in Kansas City to plan a way to convert war production industries into peace-time businesses in order to continue the region's economic growth.Out of the meeting came a suggestion that a science research center was needed in the Midwest.

Later, 24 Kansas City industrialists got together to discuss locating a permanent research facility in Kansas City. J.C. Nichols, Kenneth Spencer, and Robert Mehornay started a fund-raising effort to underwrite Midwest Research Institute. A half million dollars was pledged by 42 businesses and individuals to ensure that Kansas City would be a center of the newest scientific advances and create jobs in the sciences to expand the pool of scientific researchers.

The Institute's first offices were rented laboratory space at 40th and Pennsylvania, in what had been Westport's City Hall before that area became part of Kansas City. (The building was razed in 1955.) MRI's client and project list grew quickly. By 1951 the Institute had made enough revenue to purchase a nearby three-story building. Over the next few years MRI would expand into seven buildings scattered throughout Westport. In the first decade of operation, the staff had completed over 1,500 scientific projects from 600 companies.

In 1955 Midwest Research moved into new three-story headquarters at Volker Boulevard and Oak Street, near the campus of the University of Missouri–Kansas City. The facilities have expanded into a complex of buildings.

What started as a research facility for Midwest companies soon attracted clients from all over the world. Projects have varied from coming up with a coating so that M&M candies wouldn't melt in your hand to solving problems that threaten the environment, and research programs have investigated cancer treatment, space exploration, and solar energy, among many other topics.

According to a 1994 *Kansas City Star* article, the Institute receives 70 percent of its income from government projects, most of them for the Department of Energy and the Environmental Protection Agency.

The Camp Fire organization celebrated its 85th birthday in 1995. Although the group didn't move their headquarters to Kansas City until 1977, the city has been connected with Camp Fire's history from the beginning.

The Boy Scout movement came to America from England in 1910, but there were no planned group recreational activities in the U.S. for girls. In Vermont during 1910 a group of girls were organized to participate in summer recreational activities, often around campfires, thus the name "Camp Fire Girls." (When boys were allowed to join in 1975, the name changed to Camp Fire Boys and Girls.)

Since Boy Scout troops were organizing, sponsors of the Vermont camp and the parents of the girls who attended started making contacts with people across the country for support in putting together a national organization for girls. In 1912 Camp Fire Girls of America was incorporated as a national agency. It is one of the country's oldest and largest youth organizations.

The first Kansas City Camp Fire Girls Council was formed shortly afterwards. The first Camp Fire summer camp ever organized was held in Kansas City in 1914 at Camp Shawnee, on a farm at 81st and State Line. One hundred eighty girls participated, with tents borrowed from the Missouri National Guard. Twenty girls at a time spent one or two weeks at the camp with counselors. The next year the camp was in Grandview, Missouri. The girls enjoyed activities such as exercises, hand crafts, Bible reading, hockey or basketball, and entertainment. In the early days of the movement, many of the activities centered around Indian lore and ceremonies. In 1937 the camp was moved to the national forest near Knob Noster, Missouri.

In March 1924, with over 500 girls enrolled locally, Kansas City played host to the Camp Fire national convention. Over 4,000 girls, representing 75 cities, attended the meeting in Convention Hall. All of the Camp Fire girls marched in the parade through downtown.

The Camp Fire headquarters had always been in the East. In the early 1970s, when it was decided to move the central offices, Kansas City competed with 40 other cities for the headquarters. Kansas City was chosen because 58 percent of Camp Fire's membership lived within a 600-mile radius of the city. When the new headquarters opened at 46th and Madison in 1977, Camp Fire's membership was 500,000.

Unity School of Christianity was started in Kansas City in 1890. The founders, Myrtle and Charles Fillmore, came here from Colorado in 1884. Charles invested heavily in land development in the city's Northeast area. Soon the real estate market collapsed and he lost $150,000. The lost money and Myrtle's tuberculosis, which worsened every day, put the couple into a severe depression.

The Fillmores began reading books on the world's religions and philosophies. Through prayer, Myrtle reasoned that there was a supreme power operating within a fixed divine law. She felt that if an individual could set aside all negative and destructive thoughts, they would be in unity with that power. After a time of meditation and prayer, her tuberculosis was cured. The Fillmores dedicated themselves to this new teaching and began to hold prayer meetings with friends in their home at 1315 McGee.

In 1889 the couple started publishing their philosophy in *Modern Thought. Wee Wisdom*, a magazine for children, began in 1893. Later additional publications were added, including the popular *Daily Word.*

In 1891 Charles named the movement "Unity." In 1914 it became the Unity School of Christianity. By 1906 Unity had enough followers to construct a Unity Society building at Ninth and Tracy, just east of downtown Kansas City. In 1910 another building went up at 10th and Tracy to accommodate a school for ministers and Kansas City's first vegetarian cafe. In 1922 Unity started broadcasting from their own radio station, WOQ.

In 1920 the Fillmores purchased 50 acres of land to the east of Kansas City, near Lee's Summit, Missouri. It was first called Unity Farm and later designated as a city—Unity Village. Over the years, the acreage has expanded, and buildings have been designed and constructed to make the Village a tranquil haven. Today almost 600 Unity churches operate in the United States, with 20 others worldwide and study groups on every continent. The school at the Village trains ministers and offers a variety of workshops. Myrtle Fillmore died in 1931 and Charles in 1948. Their descendents guide Unity today.

The Nazarenes, originally part of a movement that came out of the Methodist religion and The Holiness People, shifted their headquarters to Kansas City in 1915. Their philosophy includes modesty in dress, plus no smoking, drinking, or dancing. The Church of the Nazarene purchased property at 24th and Troost, where they built a church and a publishing house. By 1923 The Nazarene Press was printing over 26 million pieces of literature. Needing more space, the group constructed a new building at 29th and Troost, where the Nazarene Publishing House still operates.

In 1954 the Church of the Nazarene moved into newly constructed headquarters at Meyer Boulevard and The Paseo. The Nazarene seminary is also located there. There are eight Church of the Nazarene liberal arts colleges across the country (one in nearby Olathe, Kansas). Today 11,133 Nazarene churches have a worldwide membership of over a million.

Kansas City has been called a "livable city" because of its green spaces, cultural activities, and friendly atmosphere. Many businesses and institutions continue to find the city ideal for their headquarters.

KANSAS CITY'S SPIRIT

Any one of the many natural or economic disasters in the city's history could have curtailed Kansas City's growth. But each time the citizenry has rallied to bring the city back stronger than ever. Some may call this civic pride, but here it is better known as "The Kansas City Spirit."

The town lost much of its population and economic stability during the Civil War. After the war Robert Van Horn, editor and publisher of the *Western Journal of Commerce* newspaper (later to become *The Journal)*, wrote, "There is a tide in the affairs of men and the same is true of cities . . . If we do not act at the tide of our opportunities, our future history will be a record of failure and humiliation." Van Horn gave the town confidence, and within four years the Hannibal Bridge had gone up. And at this point Kansas City was well on its way to becoming a railroad center, heading toward a new phase of prosperity.

Kersey Coates was a tireless worker who helped get the bridge erected, developed the Quality Hill neighborhood, and built the Coates Opera House and the Coates House hotel. But there was another leader in the family—Sarah Coates was an outspoken advocate for civic improvement and women's rights. Her husband built buildings; Sarah built lives. Before and after her husband's death, Sarah started several women's and arts clubs. She was an early advocate for voting rights, and several times entertained Susan B. Anthony, leader of the women's suffrage movement, at her home in Quality Hill.

Kersey Coates was building an addition to his hotel when he died in 1887. A portion of the structure you see today was finished by Sarah after his death. A fire in 1978 destroyed some of the hotel, but the Coates House was renovated in 1984 and is an apartment building today.

These early leaders' vision of Kansas City's potential would inspire generations of leaders who followed. William Rockhill Nelson, like Kersey Coates, developed a neighborhood, and like Robert Van Horn, used the pulpit of his newspapers to make the town better.

Nelson came to Kansas City in 1880 from Fort Wayne, Indiana, where he had been a contractor and builder and also owned the town's newspaper. He founded *The Kansas City Evening Star* in 1880 and bought *The Kansas City Times* in 1901. He used the two daily papers to get things done. Nelson wrote editorials almost every day of the need to improve the city and provide benefits for its residents. In the mid-1880s he started the crusade to get the city to provide parks for its citizens. He not only pushed the cause for parks with editorials and stories, but, he also printed letters to the editor in support, supposedly from the public but written by his staff.

The townspeople first got interested in establishing a city park in 1877, when the city decided to convert the old city graveyard at Locust and Independence Avenue into one. The cemetery had been used since the early 1840s as a burial ground for most of the early pioneers. To make the park, inmates of the city's workhouse dug up the coffins and bones and reburied them in a corner of the graveyard. New wooden tombstones were made to identify each grave, and a fence was put around the smaller burial site. The rest of the cemetery then was "beautified." It was first called Cemetery Park, and later Shelley's Park, after Mayor George Shelley. The mayor said that the park was near workingmen's neighborhoods, the city hall, and the retail district, and it hadn't cost the city a cent. This wasn't true of the parks and boulevard system that was finally put into effect in the 1890s. By the time the first phase was accomplished in 1915, the price tag was almost $15 million.

Before the city could put a park plan into motion, a new charter had to be voted on that would allow condemnation rights to acquire land for the parks. Political wrangling at both city and county levels persisted over five years before the legalities were cleared. In 1889 the city got the OK to appoint a park commission. Once one was appointed, however, there was nothing to administer, because there was no plan and no money had been collected.

In 1892 a second park board was appointed: Simeon Armour, head of the meat-packing company; William Glass, wealthy retired liquor dealer; Louis Hammerslough, a philanthropist who made a fortune manufacturing shoes; and August Meyer, who became the president of the board. Meyer and Nelson would be the driving forces behind getting the parks and boulevards plan put into motion.

Meyer helped to found the town of Leadville, Colorado, and gave the town its name. He became wealthy by starting the first ore reduction works to extract the silver from the stone dug out of the mines there. He moved to Kansas City in 1881 and opened a smelting factory in the Argentine district. Ore was shipped from the mines Meyer owned in Colorado and Mexico to the factory here so that the gold, silver, and lead could be extracted. At one time the factory employed over 1,000 workers.

Although it was reported that Meyer and Nelson went in search of George Kessler to design the parks and boulevard system, actually he came to them looking for a job. Kessler, a landscape architect who had spent some time working in New York's Central Park, came to the area in 1882. He was hired as the superintendent of parks by the Kansas City, Fort Scott and Gulf Railroad to design an amusement park on land the railroad company owned in Merriam, Kansas. He also was in charge of the landscaping around all of the railroad's depots.

Kessler opened an office in Kansas City and soon designed a small park in the middle of the Hyde Park neighborhood. As soon as Kansas City's new park board was in place, Kessler applied for a job. He was hired not as landscape architect but as "secretary" at a salary of $200 a month. But Kessler did design the park and boulevard plan in 1893, and the Kansas City's park system is still acknowledged as one of the best in the country.

Kessler's plan proposed three parks and, in order to build them, the city was divided into three property tax assessment districts. From the time the plan was presented until 1900, there was continued opposition to the levying of property taxes to support the park plan. Some homeowners called it a mortgage on their houses. Many thought the plan was too big and ambitious.

Nelson had written glowing articles in *The Star* praising Thomas Swope for his gift of park land. But a few years later, because Swope sided with those who opposed taxing vacant and undeveloped land, Nelson ridiculed him in an satirical article, making fun of him because he had failed to improve some downtown property. It was reported that Swope took such offense at the article that he went to the newspaper office and told the first person he saw to inform the publisher that if he ever saw his name in *The Star* again, he would kill Nelson. So much for Mr. Swope being called shy and reclusive.

The park plan included an area above and below the wooded, craggy limestone cliffs that face the Missouri River in the Northeast section of town. August Meyer, who rode horseback through this area, desired to keep it as natural as it had been for centuries. The area became North Terrace Park. A road known as Cliff Drive winds midway below the cliffs for three miles. The wooded area below has been left undisturbed. Unfortunately, though, a natural spring along the drive has been replaced by an artificial waterfall.

The other two parks that Kessler proposed replaced blight and slums along the top of the West Bluffs and in a ravine that later became

Penn Valley Park. Nelson said that the shacks on the West Bluffs gave the visitor arriving at the Union Depot the wrong impression of Kansas City. (However, the depot and Union Street did that before any visitor had a chance to look up.) In turning these slum areas into parks, many poor people, mostly blacks, were turned out into the cold. No provision was made to relocate them.

The plan also proposed boulevards, planted with trees and gardens, that would connect these parks and make them accessible to the public. Some called the boulevards the playgrounds of the rich, because the wealthy lived on or close to them. The parks were called the playgrounds of the poor. Kessler's boulevards were so wide that later, when the automobile was invented, the streets easily accommodated two-lane traffic and parking. In 1895 a section of Independence Avenue, from Woodland to Gladstone, was widened and paved and designated as the city's first boulevard. August Meyer lived on this thoroughfare until 1896, when he built a 26-room brick house at 44th and Warwick. The house is now the administration office for the Kansas City Art Institute.

The building of The Paseo was also influenced by Meyer. He suggested naming it after Mexico City's Paseo de la Reforma, although it more closely resembled those boulevards found in Europe. The first section of The Paseo from Independence Avenue to 18th Street was completed by the turn of the 20th century. Trees were planted along the sides of this roadway, which connected a series of lavish gardens that included fountains, pools, and benches. One of the most beautiful areas was the sunken garden at 12th Street. In 1970 The Paseo was realigned and much of the garden space eliminated.

William Rockhill Nelson made many contributions to this city. He pushed for the building of Convention Hall and its rebuilding after the fire. He helped to organize a group to plan for Union Station. In 1897 he donated his reproductions of famous paintings and sculptures to the city's first public art gallery. These works were exhibited in the Kansas City Public Library building on Ninth Street in a special room for 36 years.

In 1900 Nelson built his home, Oak Hall, on 20 acres running from Brush Creek to 45th Street and Oak Street to Rockhill Road. Nelson died in 1915. His will stipulated that his newspapers were to be sold and proceeds used to build an art gallery. Oak Hall was left to his wife and daughter with instructions that at their deaths the house was to be razed and the property used for an art museum. The Nelson-Atkins Museum of Art opened December 10, 1933, standing on Nelson's property. The Nelson

William Rockhill Nelson's art collection was exhibited at the Western Gallery of Art at the Kansas City Public Library at Ninth and Locust.

Trust money was used to buy paintings throughout the world for exhibition at the new museum.

J. C. Nichols was involved in almost every significant achievement of Kansas City from 1905, when he bought his first land for development, until his death in 1950. It is surprising that he had any time and energy left over to develop his housing districts and the Country Club Plaza.

Nichols was one of the original trustees for the William Rockhill Nelson trust that oversaw the building of the art gallery. He served as president of the early Art Institute and was on the Kansas City School Board. He was president of the committee that chose the site for the Liberty Memorial. He helped form the Missouri River Navigation Association in the 1930s, which got the river channel widened so that commercial barges could use the waterway.

In 1926 President Calvin Coolidge appointed J.C. Nichols as one of the four city planners on the National Park and Planning Commission. He spent 22 years on the commission that was not only responsible for looking after the planing of new parks in the country, but picked the site for the Lincoln and Jefferson monuments and the Washington Mall.

During the Second World War, Nichols was appointed to the Advisory Council for National Defense. He found that there was no plan to locate a defense plant in this part of the country. He lobbied the Congress and was instrumental in getting two munitions factories and two aircraft plants established in this area. A small boat and landing craft plant was also located on the Kaw River. These plants ran shifts around the clock, employing tens of thousands of local workers and attracting many from surrounding towns looking for jobs. A large number of those workers stayed in Kansas City after the war and expanded the city's population.

But Nichols is best known here for his Country Club Plaza. In 1906, when he was bringing people to look at the houses he was building, he had to take them through the land on the north side of Brush Creek that was a swamp, a pig farm, and a trash dump. Feeling that this would reflect on his property, he started to acquire this land in 1907. He drained the swamp and got rid of the unsightly trash and pig farm. Nichols would end up spending a million dollars for the land on which he would eventually build The Plaza.

In designing The Plaza, he solicited input from George Kessler. When he announced his plans in the newspapers, some city leaders labeled it as "Nichols Folly" because it was too far from downtown and too far from most residential areas.

Looking west from Main Street, The Plaza in the early 1930s. The J. C. Nichols Memorial Fountain is now located in the foreground.

The Plaza's first building was completed and occupied in 1923. That year, while attending the International Housing Conference in Europe, Nichols bought more than 100 sculptured art objects and had them shipped to Kansas City. He would place these in and around The Plaza and in his housing developments. He continued to acquire statues and fountains, as did his son, Miller Nichols. The Plaza with its many fountains has added to Kansas City's reputation as "The City of Fountains" and the claim that it has more fountains than Rome.

More Plaza buildings were constructed and more businesses and shops moved into them. Shoppers came from all over the city by automobile and bus. Some people came just to see and be seen.

For the 1925 Christmas season, a single strand of colored lights was hung above the Plaza's first building. Each year as more buildings were constructed, they too were outlined with bright lights at Christmas. Today the Plaza Lighting Ceremony has become a Thanksgiving evening tradition. Another annual event, the Plaza Art Fair, started in the fall of 1932 and is still one of the biggest art fairs in the Midwest.

Although J.C. Nichols accomplished many things in his lifetime, perhaps it is The Plaza, which continues to grow and change, that best exemplifies the energy and vitality of a man who saw a pig farm and a trash dump and envisioned a unique shopping experience.

William Volker not only became one of the town's earliest benefactors, he set the tone for giving in Kansas City. He gave millions away, and to so many causes anonymously that we probably never will know how many individuals and groups benefited from his generosity. He was a shy man who refused to talk about himself when questioned by reporters. The press often referred to him as "Mr. Anonymous."

Volker's family immigrated from Germany to Chicago in 1871, just in time to witness the great Chicago fire. The blaze wiped out three and a half miles of the city's central business district, killed 300 people, and left 90,000 homeless. William Volker, who was 12 at the time, never forgot the human misery that he saw and said that this influenced his lifelong compassion for those in need.

At 14 Volker quit school to go to work in a dry goods store, making a dollar a week. He was ambitious and enrolled in business college to study accounting. The illiterate owner of a thriving picture frame business hired the young Volker at $12.50 a week to be a bookkeeper and handle all of the company's correspondence. He did such a good job that when the owner was unexpectedly killed in an accident, his family asked

Volker to run the business. He was 20 years old at this time.

In a few years Volker had saved $3,000. He wanted to open a picture framing factory of his own in a city that didn't have one but offered transportation to ship his frames all over the country. Since Kansas City did not have a picture frame company, he moved here in 1882.

Volker opened his small factory on the upper floors of a building on Delaware near the City Market. His picture frames were soon being sold all over the Midwest. Later he expanded his operation to make window shades. And the small factory became a larger one that was making Volker rich. To reward those who worked for him, in 1889 he started a profit-sharing plan for his employees. He opened branches of his company across the country and by the turn of the 20th century, when he was only in his early forties, Volker was a millionaire.

William Volker used his fortune to help others. Some of his gifts were public. He gave money and land to establish a center for tuberculosis at General Hospital in 1907. He donated a building and $30,000 to the Helping Hand Institute that assisted the homeless. While he was on the Kansas City School Board between 1912 and 1926, he gave money for various school programs as well as $100,000 to establish the teachers' retirement fund.

Volker gave money to several hospitals and to help establish the city's Board of Public Welfare. He donated to the Kansas City Zoo, the Philharmonic Orchestra, and in 1930 to the establishment of a university here. The amount of that donation exceeded $2.5 million in 1930s funds. The money was used to start and sustain Kansas City University, which would later merge into the University of Missouri system.

Today's philanthropists have foundations that are staffed with people who handle requests. Those in need would approach Volker directly, however. He would often tell them, "The money can probably be found somewhere." And it almost always was. When people tried to thank him, he said he was only doing his duty. He established the William Volker Charities Fund, and at his death in 1949 it was worth $15 million.

Volker's philosophy was embedded in his statement, "The rich man is merely the custodian of his money and . . . the real reason he has it is so he may use it for the benefit of others."

Robert A. Long was another successful businessman who gave away millions. No one knows the extent of what he gave because he didn't want anyone to know. Born in Kentucky, Long came to the Midwest in 1874 and started a small lumber business. In 1884, with two partners, he founded the

Long-Bell Lumber Company in Kansas. The firm moved their offices to Kansas City in 1891. The company would eventually become one of the two largest lumber operations in the country. Before he suffered severe losses in the Depression, R.A. Long's personal wealth was estimated at $50 million.

In 1907 Robert Long built the R.A. Long Building at 10th and Grand. And in 1911 he built his home, a 70-room mansion on Gladstone Boulevard in the Northeast section of Kansas City, today home of the Kansas City Museum. Between 1912 and 1914 Long constructed 42 buildings on over 1,600 acres of Longview Farm near Lee's Summit. This was where his daughter, Loula Long Combs, raised and trained championship horses that won her blue ribbons in horse shows all over the world.

Robert Long was chairman of the one-week effort to raise $2 million to build the Liberty Memorial. He donated $70,000 to start off the campaign, and when, at the end of the week, the drive was short $70,000, he wrote another check for that amount. He gave the land and the money to build the Independence Boulevard Christian Church. It was said that Long gave money away in lavish fashion.

After the stock market crash, Long's fortune was almost wiped

R. A. Long helped raise $2 million in one week to build the Liberty Memorial. On November 11, 1926, over 100,000 people attended its dedication.

out. At 82 he successfully fought a court-battle attempt to put his lumber company into receivership. He died in 1934. Robert Long once said "I've always been a dreamer; but they have given me much pleasure, these dreams and air castles."

EPILOGUE

Each era of Kansas City's history has produced leaders who dream of what can be accomplished. Such special people are not only those high on the civic ladder. When faced with a challenge, in the tradition established by the first settlers, many ordinary people have come forward to help Kansas City achieve extraordinary things.

As this city moves into the 21st century, we can look back at all that has been accomplished and look forward with confidence to what is yet to be. That is the Kansas City spirit.

A picture of Kansas City today taken from the riverfront where it all started.
Photo by David Remley

ABOUT THE AUTHOR

This is Dory DeAngelo's fifth book about Kansas City's history. In the last ten years, besides writing books, Dory has had over 150 articles published about the city's history in various newspapers and magazines. She appeared on Channel 41 monthly for two years as a Kansas City historian, and frequently gives speeches on the subject to various groups. Dory's historic research ability has assisted authors and screen and television writers across the country, as well as clients from many other professions. In 1994 and 1995 she did research for two major Kansas City books: the biography of Ewing Kauffman and a history of Hospital Hill.

Dory, a native Kansas Citian has spent considerable time working for the city's professional theaters. "The city's history is like a grand stage full of comedy and drama, colorful characters, and captivating situations," she says. "It's a show that has to be shared."